NOT SET IN STONE

*For everyone who helped.
You know who you are and
I wouldn't be here without you.*

NOT SET IN STONE

The passion and consequence of a mountain life

DAVID VASS

pb potton & burton

Published with the generous
support of the Federated
Mountain Clubs Mountain
and Forest Trust.

First published in 2023
by Potton & Burton

Potton & Burton
319a Hardy Street,
PO Box 221, Nelson, New Zealand

© David Vass

ISBN 978 1 98 855050 3

Editing: Anna Rogers

Printed in New Zealand by Blue Star

CONTENTS

A Beginning

It could start like this, as many things do, with getting out of the car. Right away you can feel it – the world as a much bigger place, the car a confinity, separate from what you've now stepped into. Forest rises all around the carpark and beyond that mountains. You breathe deeply, and the sounds are no longer of your journey but of arrival: the noisy stones in the nearby river, the calling of birds. The air is fresh and moving. There is a track into the forest. You follow it and soon turn a corner, skirt a large tree and the road has gone. The sounds are now much reduced, as if the forest keeps things out, and at the same time you also feel smaller, as if it absorbs things too.

You walk slowly because it takes a while to feel at home within this new world. It takes the appearance of a clearing, some sun shining on a root that looks like a seat, to encourage you to sit among the trees for a while; some light from the outside world to remind you that there's more than just otherness here, that it's okay to be part of it.

Words spring to mind: dappled, twitter, hush. Your eyes are drawn further in, to a scene of sorts, where a fantail flits around in a sunny patch and there is an old log covered in moss. You stand and look further along the track and then back to the fantail, the sun, the mossy log. It looks somehow more interesting, so that's where you go; you leave the track.

You are now within the forest, rather than passing through it. Travel becomes more physical. You need to use your hands to push through the vegetation and the ground beneath you becomes more uneven, your foot placements more considered.

The sounds around you become closer: the flutter of the robin picking up the insects you disturb, the brush of vegetation against your clothing, your feet snapping twigs underfoot and sinking into the moss, the sounds of your body itself. Your breath.

You stay only briefly in the small clearing because almost immediately there's something else to see: a tiny watercourse snaking through the moss and a grove of ferns, the papery bark of a tree fuchsia, some bright flower pods lying on the ground. Then, the knotted trunk of an old tree.

Running the palm of your hand over the trunk, you feel solidity, a sense of age. A big tree will always draw the eye upwards and there is a world there, a hanging platform of greenery at the first forking of branches. From where you stand, a sturdy vine, just the right size to grip securely with your hands, snakes up to the platform. The trunk is angled back somewhat – it really wouldn't be too hard to get up there. It's easy to imagine the view.

Tentatively, you test the vine and it feels even more secure than you had imagined. You look around, perhaps to convince yourself that it's okay to be doing this and the soft-mounded moss around the base of the tree seems to confirm it. You take off your shoes; your toes curl and grip the sharp flakes of bark. There is a moment, as you try to get onto the platform, that you need to sink your fingers deep into the humus to gain purchase for the final heave into the heart of the tree.

Once there, you quiver with aliveness – a kind of exultation – even as another part of your mind is wondering how the climb down will go. That doesn't matter though, because no one has ever been to the place you're now in, and it is beautiful. This, just this simple action, has brought you to a place that is all yours to be part of. From the branches you sit within, there is a view further up the valley, to where the bush gives way to more open country. Beyond that, tussock slopes angle up to great walls of rock, some of which rise to snowy heights, some so cold they are streaked with ice, some so high they disappear into cloud. A breeze stirs through the tree, moves the branches you stand on, pushes the clouds across the sky. Perhaps, just perhaps, this is how something begins.

I stand at the bottom of the chairlift, wearing my shabby outdoor gear and old daypack, ice axe in hand. Around me, well-dressed skiers schuss past and queue for the lift, eyeing me briefly before being whisked up the mountain and into the cloud. I feel something of an oddity; there are plenty of other high-school kids here, but they're all here to ski. Penniless students don't ride chairlifts so I start walking. It's 1978. I've never climbed a mountain before.

Whakapapa ski field, high on the flanks of Mount Ruapehu, is a busy place. I hike up slowly, trying not to get in the way of the brightly clad skiers. The lifts clank loudly. A skidoo roars past, leaving fumes in its wake. I carry on past a bustling cafe and another queue waiting for the next chairlift. The cloud thickens. Skiers appear briefly out of the gloom to disappear again down the hill, making wet sliding noises as they pass.

Eventually, beyond the ski field, there are no more people. There are also no features to keep perspective in the mist, and I stumble on through a disorienting whiteout, the noises fading behind me. The snow is soft and wet on top, full of cloud moisture, and the murk continues to thicken. I start to lose my bearings on the wide slopes, until even the sense of uphill direction has gone. Alarmingly wobbly in the uniform whiteness, I sit down on the snow to take in the quiet around me. After a time there's a faint lightening, the sense that somewhere above me is sunshine.

I am born into another world of brightness and glare, of frozen water and blue clear sky; it seems incredibly pure. Once my squinted eyes adjust to the light I can see for miles, the volcanic cone of Taranaki proud in the distance. There is an ocean of cloud at my feet, a uniformly smooth blanket that covers the landscape in every direction. It seems incongruous that such breathtaking quiet and clarity should exist so separately from what lies under the cloud.

The snow underfoot is mixed with harder patches of ice and I stop to fix crampons to my boots, the first time I've used them other than in practice. Although I'm in the sun, the temperature is below freezing and the snow, when kicked, is a loose and sparkling dust. Ice features rise out of the snow, shaped by the wind into strange gargoyles.

Within a short time the view over the rest of the mountain unfolds before me. I see there is much more up here than I had ever envisaged. It is a realisation I am to make again and again throughout my mountain life. Below me lies the crater lake, muddied and blue, poured into the folds of the mountain, steam rising quietly from its tepid waters. Rising above, the peaks of Te Heuheu and Tukino ring the summit area of Ruapehu and the sharp triangle of Pyramid rises from the centre. My eye is drawn around the summit ridge and a thrill runs through me as an idea gels in my mind: today I will climb all of them.

To my right the ridge I'm on drops to a saddle before rising, via an icy ridge, to Tahurangi, the main summit of Ruapehu. I can't help but head to the highest point first, enjoying the security the crampons provide, the feel of grip on a frozen surface. The ridge to the summit is a divider between two very different types of terrain. On the sheltered side a smooth snow slope drops towards the lake. On the windswept southern side, the face is a maze of twisted rime-ice formations. The easy way is obvious but I'm drawn to the icier side; it just looks more interesting. After traversing around from the saddle for a while, I imagine I see a line that rises all the way toward the summit. For the first time, a collection of physical features calls my name.

I start up, crampons biting into the ice, and the slope quickly steepens enough to get onto my front points. I find myself stuck into the mountain on two slender spikes of steel, balancing on my toes. I am now using the pick of the ice axe as well, which adds to the feeling of actually climbing.

As the ice steepens, I am forced to be more creative with my feet, taking my body weight on the platform they make so I can remove the pick and reposition it above me. The climbing becomes increasingly interesting and the higher I climb, the more committed I become.

In the kicking of cramponed feet and the swinging of the ice axe,
I start to get the feel of what it is to be climbing a mountain; the sense
of removal from the world, of doing something special, if only to me.
Towards the top, the runnel rolls over to form an enclosed tube of ice
and I have to resort to wriggling up within its confines. It's wildly good
fun and, to top it off, I pop out of the tube right at the top.

In retrospect, Ruapehu – my first snowy peak – was the perfect
summit. There was a kind of purity to it. I had no real plans on the day;
no map, no expectations. I was on my own with no sign of anyone else,
just me and a bright, high world. Everything felt new, and the blanket of
cloud below hid the rest of the world from me and me from it. It was an
exhilaration to be there. I laughed out loud, often.

From the top I plot my route before setting off, sullying the pristine
slopes with my tracks, down to the crater lake. One day I'll be a skier,
but not yet. It's slightly eerie being down at lake level. A large ice bulge
hangs over the water at the far end and an obvious wave-worn overhang
rings the edge. It feels as though I shouldn't hang around there too
long. My caution is justified. As I'm scratching my way carefully above
the lake, a large chunk of the ice bulge falls off into the crater, sending
a wave across the lake that crashes hard into the overhang. This
causes me to feel even more tenuous. The lake belches and gurgles in a
sulphurous manner below me. I feel small, an alien presence in a place
where I'm not sure I belong.

The day progresses. I learn to use my crampons, and my axe, on
different angles and terrain, begin to get a feel for this new style of
movement. My sweat dries chilly on me whenever I stop and my toes are
cold all day. My breath hangs in the breathless air, the sun feels like an
illumination rather than a heater, and everywhere below me the cloud
sits like a shroud over the land.

After a day of travelling, I've seen no sign of anyone, and it seems
that this is how I like it. I sit on the saddle below Te Heuheu, the last of

the peaks I will climb today. The sun is lowering toward the horizon, near to the distant triangle of Taranaki. Below me the cloud is finally breaking up and glimpses of the ski field, and the way down, are revealed. Soon it will be dark but I remain sitting, reluctant to return.

Over the plateau of Mount Ruapehu, the blue shadows are growing longer and the light is starting to colour. The cloud blanket, side-lit now, is made of iridescent blue valleys sitting among vibrant yellow hillsides, an otherworldly landscape floating above the real earth. The temperature is dropping back below freezing, but I can't look away. Already, I know that I will keep returning to places like this, that there will be more.

When I arrive back later that evening, quietly chuffed with my adventure, my parents ask how my day was. It turns out that I'm unable to talk, my throat dried out and raspy, to add to the oddity of my sunburnt face and a mind that is elsewhere. A thumbs-up and appreciation of a large dinner are all I can muster.

After leaving school in Rotorua, I moved down south to study biology at Canterbury University and immediately found myself on the edge of a world that seemed made for adventure. Within striking distance of Christchurch there were mountains, rivers and coastlines in abundance to explore. Early on, my strategy for learning the ways of the outdoor world was to head out into the hills as often as I could, with whoever was keen. There were plenty of other enthusiasts, and thanks to a university schedule of maximum flexibility with plenty of holidays, I was out there often. The characters I first came across were a bunch of engineering school types, who had a knack for dreaming up and instigating a range of oddball activities in the outdoors, which seemed largely created to have fun. The mountains would have to wait.

The first of these outings was a descent of the Buller River, over four days, in whatever kind of craft we could manufacture.

The most memorable consisted of about a dozen tyre tubes tied together in a haphazard way, a kind of an unstable bouncy castle that tended to randomly turn turtle when it hit turbulence and toss its inhabitants into the river. As the stricken crew tried to haul themselves back onboard, the craft would invariably overbalance and roll onto them, creating a dynamic and endlessly humorous descent of pretty much every rapid.

The first day passed without undue incident and it wasn't until the bottom of the first major Class IV rapid, Granity, on the second day, that I became properly aware of Dave. With a background of pulling engines apart and fixing stuff, he had never done any kind of river boating and, having just survived Granity on some sort of makeshift craft, said something like 'Shit, that was fun', returned to the top, jumped eagerly back into the river and swam the length of the rapid. He emerged, having spent some time being thrashed around in the final hole, looking somewhat beaten up but well satisfied with his adventure. This was a look I would come to know well over the next couple of years.

PART ONE

LIMESTONE

Limestone has a different origin to the inorganic sources of most other rock types. It has its genesis in the remains of living things, specifically the detritus of the shells of billions of sea creatures squashed under their own weight: right from the start, it's different. If an acid-crazed mad scientist were to design a type of stone, the outcome would most likely resemble limestone, in that it forms structures and shapes unlike any other stone. It's the novelty rock of the geological world.

Limestone has one particular quality that allows this to happen: it is soluble in water. This means that the centuries it usually takes for water to erode a rock are compressed into a shorter period. As well as wearing away at the rock, water also dissolves limestone and the results are spectacular. Rounded features are especially popular – pockets and potholes, crazy overhangs – and no other rock forms stalactites. Given a bit of time and a bit of water, limestone can form the oddest of features, but nothing is stranger than caves and all they contain. Except perhaps, for the motivations of the people who explore them.

Caves with Dave

Dave was big – big, strong and exuding a strong air of invincibility. He also possessed an extraordinarily high tolerance for suffering, usually with a goofy grin plastered on his face. These qualities made him a prime candidate for the next activity we embarked on.

Caving is a sport for the enthusiast and for a couple of years Dave and I were just that. Caving requires a certain motivation – some would say perversity. It also requires that, rather than just putting up with discomfort, you embrace it, particularly the filth, grit, cold, hard work and slime that are your constant companions underground. Dave and I were drawn to the only aspect of this sport that made any sense to us – exploratory caving. Motivation was never discussed. It was a given: the unknown.

Before I met Dave, I'd been caving twice. At the end of the first trip, in some obscure cave system near Lake Te Anau, I swore I would never do it again. We had gotten lost, badly, and spent several hours duckwalking or crawling on our knees through a maze of identical tubes little more than a metre high. The one room that apparently contained nice formations, we never found. I'd become scared when my light went out while I was wriggling through a tight watery bit by myself, and we had all ended up cold and very wet. My caving mentor, Al, assured me this was all pretty normal.

On my second trip, I spent four continuous days underground in the Nettlebed system, a complicated and extensive array of watercourses deep in the limestone of north-west Nelson beneath the massif of Mount Arthur. Not far into the cave, I had spent several hours passing the contents of our packs through a series of the tightest squeezes I could imagine, back and forth through the tightest one – a z-shaped tube that required a 90-degree twist to negotiate – until the gnawing sickness of claustrophobia had waned. I had then been roundly abused by an enraged old-school caver type for being 'hopelessly underprepared and incompetent for a serious cave like this one', when, most of a long day into the cave, he discovered Al teaching me how to jumar at the bottom of a long rope ascent. When I reached the campsite later that day, I discovered that my sleeping bag, part of the permanent stash in the cave, was full of mould. Al just shrugged.

A couple of long, tiring and continually dark days later, though, we found ourselves sitting in a chamber, known as the Rubik Room, its floor consisting of large sharp-edged and symmetrical blocks. To get there, we had abseiled the walls of vertical shafts, traversed galleries of glittering crystal pools and seen flowing columns of water that had turned to marble. At one stage we had struggled up through a long choke of wedged boulders and, on emerging into the bottom of a large chamber, had turned our lamps on full and shone them upwards towards a roof that wasn't there. The vault was so large our lights couldn't reach the end, as if we had emerged into the night of another world.

Sitting there among the blocks, we were aware that our time in the cave was coming to an end. The Rubik Room was then, in the 1980s, the end of the explored terrain of Nettlebed. Anything we found from here would be new, not just to us but to anyone, and in front of us was a large, promising-looking hole set high in a vertical face. The wall up to it looked difficult, and without the appropriate gear or the time, we would have to return another time. That's all it takes – to wonder where a hole might go to, and what could possibly be in there.

A lot of water travels through the porous veins of Mount Arthur, before exiting at the deep upwelling of the Pearce Resurgence. This promised an enormous amount of new terrain, with large streamways and passages to explore. It was thought, and surveys had shown, that the Nettlebed system might potentially join up with another steep and dramatic system higher up within the mountain, known somewhat prosaically as HH, after a trig station somewhere near the alpine-level entrance to the cave. If the two caves could be made into one, it would create the deepest navigable through-trip in the southern hemisphere. We had been to the end of Nettlebed and we had seen that hole in the wall. We were keen.

Reality doesn't always match expectation. Some two months later we sat, Al, Dave, Pat and I, on those same rocks in the Rubik Room, looking at the same hole in the wall. Same hole but not the same, because now there was a rope hanging out of it. Someone had beaten us to it.

We made the effort and climbed up the rope and it was only a slight relief to discover that the passage beyond didn't go anywhere particularly exciting. As you do at such times, we sat down for a cup of tea and something to eat. I stretched out over a boulder while Dave went fossicking under the rocks for some dropped utensil. I think we all dozed off for a while.

When we woke it took a while for someone to ask where Dave had gone. This was unsurprising: Dave wasn't the lie around and snooze type. We were, though, starting to wonder when we first heard the sounds of his return, deep down in the boulders beneath our feet: first the scrabble of rocks shifting on one other, then heavy breathing and the sounds of effort and eventually, for he was a long way below us, Dave himself emerged, scratched, sweaty, a goofy grin on his face and clutching his Swiss army knife.

'There's adventure to be had,' he said, or words to that effect. It seemed that the floor of the chamber we were in was in fact a false floor jammed over the top of a gigantic chasm, which Dave suggested we promptly get down to and explore.

Crawling through boulder chokes is a funny business; grovelly, uncomfortable and potentially dangerous. Each rock is supported by the one below and the ones around it, and gravity seems an essential yet dangerously precarious ingredient. There's no pattern to the way the rocks are jammed together, and among the tightness and discomfort, no pattern of movement that works better than another. The main skill is in avoiding the movement that will dislodge some supporting stone – perhaps shifting what often seems a delicate balance – and bring the whole lot down to trap you, or one of the other terrible scenarios that are hard to banish from your mind in these places.

Below the last of the boulders lay a deep blackness and the test stones we dropped took several seconds to reach the bottom. The abseil took us down between the vertical walls of a spectacular rift. As I descended, I looked back up the rope I was hanging on. The jammed boulders we'd crawled through were poised above our heads and it was easy to imagine that the rope was anchored to the one, the keystone, that would bring it all down upon us. I wondered if I should crack this joke, but didn't. We touched down in a small streamway and it occurred to me, maybe for the first time in my life, that no one had ever been here before. I could see the realisation in Dave too.

Almost immediately the little stream joined a much larger one and excitement levels reached a new peak. Stream passages are the most likely to go somewhere and provide good travel and this one, excitingly, came from the right direction – from HH. Pat and Al went downstream and we went up and I still remember the feeling of taking those first steps up the stream, of the huge potential of the world that we were right at the edge of, and not knowing how much more of it might be out there.

In the end it didn't come to much. After 100 metres or so the main stream flowed out of an impenetrable rockfall. Many passages were blocked by zones of pulverised rock and we ended up prospecting into less and less likely terrain, until the constantly loose rock started to wear on our enthusiasm. Eventually we were left with only one option, an elevated and unlikely opening set high in the side wall of the main streamway. Dave, still enthusiastic of course, murmured something about having a look, which I dismissed through tiredness and frayed nerves. I went off for a last scout of the area to make sure we hadn't missed anything, already feeling the let-down and also how very far it was back to somewhere comfortable and friendly.

I had just left Dave when there was a loud crash of rocks falling behind me and a body-hitting-the-ground noise, followed by a silence that was deepened by the knowledge that, should one of us be seriously injured, at this far end of a particularly inaccessible bit of cave, we might as well be on the moon. Dave was lying flat on his back on the marble floor of the streambed, surrounded by jagged rocks. He had missed landing on every one of them, and every one that had fallen with him, had missed him also. He was glaring down at one rock in particular. It was about the size of a coffee table, and had not crushed his leg only because it had been held up by two other fortuitous rocks either side of him.

'That's the bastard that pulled off on me,' he said as he dragged himself out from under it and dusted himself off. Looking at his landing spot, I could almost imagine an indent of his body in the hard stone floor, and the errant flake feeling like it had earned a stern telling off. We returned to the surface, having spent a monochrome week underground, and we did so at dawn, into a riot of colour and birdsong. We had not found many new passages but we had found some, and that was enough. Dave and I were heading to HH.

HH was completely different from any other cave – well, the other two – that I'd been in. It is a wild serpent of a thing that snakes through the secret body of Mount Arthur, vertically down until the water it contains reaches the water table in the lower Nettlebed system and exits at the Pearce Resurgence. From the 65-metre entrance shaft high on the mountain, the cave stays almost continually vertical for eight long and complex rope lengths, at the end of which there is an area of horizontal development and the cave's closest proximity to the explored reaches of Nettlebed.

Below this level, the cave had been explored only once that we knew of and it sounded spectacular. From the campsite level, a series of smaller abseils apparently arrived at a monstrous shaft and a pitch known as the More-rope pitch, because the first person down had to call for more rope to reach the bottom of the shaft. From then on the route continued steeply down a watercourse, via increasingly sketchy abseils and a couple of water squeezes to a termination in a sump, where the water level reached the roof and which the first descentionists, already pretty strung out, were unable to get past.

From this point, of course, there is only one way to get back out of the cave – back the way you've come. A vertical cave is hard work. For one thing, climbing up ropes, usually vertical or free hanging, is strenuous, and from the lower reaches of HH back to the surface is around 700 vertical metres of jumaring. For another thing, all the rope you require must be carried in and, at the end of the trip, out again. Normally, a trip like this would require the all hands on deck approach of an expedition, but I figured the good broad shoulders of Dave could carry a lot of stuff.

One feature of HH, however, transcends even the Dave advantage, and that's water, specifically the water that is the waterfall on the fifth pitch (pitches being numbered from the top down). The abseil down the fifth, directly and unavoidably follows the waterfall – not that great an obstacle until it rains, when the force of the water makes it impossible to climb back up the rope. Our friend Greg had once spent four hungry days in the cave, waiting for the water to go down. In the stream passage of the lower cave, the consequences could be even more serious – much of the passage floods to the roof. And therein lies the rub for multi-day caving in an area like north-west Nelson – it can rain. And, days into the cave, you won't know it.

We had travelled to Mount Arthur from Christchurch, in Dave's home-built beach buggy, which he'd knocked up around the chassis of an old

Morris 1100. It had bucket seats (two) and you needed to wear warm clothing since it was an open cockpit affair. All the packs full of rope and gear, an awful lot of it, were piled high on the back. It took two very heavy carries over a couple of days to get it all to the cave entrance. It would've been three without Dave, who was apologising for not being able to carry more as he was feeling a bit under the weather. Dropping down the first abseil, a spectacular vertical shaft, was something of a relief from the exertion, but lowering and shepherding the large packs down the rappels and terrain in between was an arduous and time-consuming activity on the unfamiliar terrain.

It wasn't until around the top of the fourth pitch that I realised all was not well with Dave, when he started vomiting. Despite this, we carried on, lugging the packs and lowering the gear down the next pitch until it became obvious that we had to stop. We sat around for a while, the sound of the fifth pitch waterfall below us in the darkness. More sickness ensued, so we left the gear there and began the long climb out, me hoping like hell he wouldn't collapse so I would have to haul him out. He didn't collapse, but he did keep on spewing. As he ascended the entrance pitch, I held the rope taut from below to make it slightly easier for him. The evening light sent a blue beam down the centre of the shaft. Dave, crawling up the suspended thread of the rope in his steaming overalls, with his Cyclops headlamp, seemed like an alien spider being beamed up, ever so slowly, to some other planet.

The start of the next attempt had a better feel to it. We had spent a few days recuperating around Nelson, much of the gear was already in the cave and we felt as though we knew our way around a bit. I had also devised a cunning plan to bypass the waterfall. Optimism reigned. We had the idea, too, that we wouldn't take a timepiece. On our week in Nettlebed the previous year, we had quite naturally slipped into longer day cycles of around 36 hours – long days of exploring followed by long stints in our sleeping bags. We had enjoyed the timeless element of this, so resolved to just let things take their course and see how long it all took. We would have no idea of what the hour, or even the day, might be.

It all seemed pretty exciting, with our light packs, no time pressures and a bit of a head start, but leaving the beauty of a sunlit alpine afternoon for the close dark of an extended night still took an effort of will.

The fourth and fifth pitches of HH are actually one long continuous chasm, with the waterfall entering halfway down. I had resolved, on the last trip, to use the amount of swing I could generate on a long rope, to pendulum high across the top of the waterfall and place a new anchor. This would mean that we could rig the rope out to the side of the waterfall and remove the nagging 'what if' scenario of being stuck in the cave if it rained.

The re-rig went well for starters. I managed to swing wide across the right-hand wall and place a tiny sky-hook over a small edge. This enabled me to hang in place and hand-drill the bolt placements we needed to redirect the ropes. It took a while, though, and it was a big, dark and atmospheric place to work. Finally, at the end of a long stint on the rope, I ended up in the waterfall for only the last few metres of the descent.

After Dave had lowered the bags and I'd dragged them out of the pool at the bottom, I looked back up the waterfall, tracing the line of the rope back up into the darkness. In my mind's eye I could see the ropes we had rigged so far continuing in a single strand, a fine and near continuous line of connection back to the surface, which already, seemed a long way from where I stood. I was already impressed at the scale of this place, its near continuous verticality and sheer size; arriving at the top of pitch eight sometime later, I was even more impressed.

A single bolt anchored the rope above a narrow slot, too small to fit through with a pack attached and not particularly impressive looking. I clipped in and lowered myself to the constriction. It took an effort to wriggle myself through the gap, and I positively popped out from a narrow fissure into the space below. I hung from the exact apex of a huge domed vault, like a tiny lightbulb in the roof of the world. My lights weren't strong enough to illuminate the ground or the walls around me, and the rope hung free below me into darkness. As I descended the rope, I felt smaller than ever.

The next 'day', Dave and I decided to head on down the main streamway for a look. We came first to the More-rope pitch – a prosaic name for such a magnificent feature. Already some 400 metres underground, the stream we were following dropped down a vertical shaft over 100 metres deep. As we abseiled, we could see that the side walls were hung with pointed stalactites that seeped from horizontal cracks, so that looking back up, it felt as though we were in a long throat ringed with internal fangs. The idea of an earthquake – some kind of shudder in the underworld – to dislodge them and send a rain of giant daggers down on us was easy to imagine, especially when hanging there on the slender thread of our lifeline. These are the sort of thoughts that occur to you dark, deep in the earth.

After the drama of More-rope, the streamway flattened and narrowed up. As we scrambled down, we noticed evidence of flooding up to the roof of the chamber. Dave, during some awkward manoeuvre, had dislocated his shoulder – an old injury that he put back in without too much ado. We continued, the shoulder came out again and painkillers were taken. Dave started to look a little beaten up but still cheerful and so we kept going – operating under some kind of 'this is not tiddlywinks/we've come all this way' motivation, – until we came to the first water squeeze.

This to us was a feature of some mythology. Only one party we knew of had been here; we had no concrete information and its physical shape had been the source of much conjecture. The obviously narrow tube into which the stream ran looked unpleasant, but beyond that, it was hard to tell what happened in there. I would have suggested Dave maybe having a go, except that he was again putting his shoulder back in place. He did helpfully suggest, though, that I should just carry on by myself – even if just for a look – and we could come back when his shoulder felt better.

I only started to really regret this decision once there was no going back – when I was lying on my side in a tube so tight that I needed my helmet off, one arm out in front, and was only able to proceed in very small and gruelling increments. That was the squeeze part, and all was okay until it came to the water bit: with my head jammed between my arm and the roof of the tube, the water started to come up to the level of my mouth, and in a sickening rise of claustrophobic panic, I realised it was now physically impossible to reverse. All I could do was keep going – slowly and calmly – because you can't get through tight squeezes if you start freezing up halfway through.

On the other side, I had little desire to continue on my own, and even less enthusiasm for getting back into the tightness and returning. Sitting in the small pool of light from my headlamp, I felt completely alone and deeper in the earth than I had ever been. I turned my lamp off and sat for a time, the burble of the stream the only sound, the darkness profound. This was as far as we would get on this trip and this moment before turning around seemed worth marking, this moment of connection with the earth worth savouring.

You can only be so happy, though, knowing that an untimely rise in the stream level will lead to your doom, and my explorations beyond the squeeze were quick. As Dave had correctly prophesied, the water rose even higher on my face during the return. Dave wasn't looking quite so perky either, but all the way back up the climbs in the streamway, and all the way back up the rope on the More-rope pitch, with its hanging daggers made all the more bizarre by the shifting lights from our headlamps, and all the long and strange and difficult way back to camp, he never complained about anything, although it obviously hurt like hell.

After a long night's sleep we decided our time in the cave had come to an end. We hadn't found much new terrain, but we'd had a great time and were ready to derig and leave. The long task of exiting the cave began.

The water level in the stream has risen by the time we arrive at the bottom of the fifth pitch waterfall and the first 10 metres of ascent involve being pummelled by the waterfall, the force strong enough to push me in and out of the flow. This is repeated several times before I gain enough height to get past the flow and it is a slow but exciting start to the pitch. Dave is on the ropes somewhere below me and I'm nearing the anchors at the top of pitch four, resting in my harness, when it happens. I'll never forget the noise.

The chamber below me fills with the roar of falling rock smashing into the ground, and among it there is a scream, and it takes a long time for it to die away, as if the sound were trying to escape somewhere to be heard, but it couldn't. The silence that follows seems as profound as the chaos of the noise; I almost dare not call out in case there's no response and sickeningly, when I try repeatedly, there isn't. I change onto my abseil device and descend back to the top of the fifth pitch. More yelling into the huge darkness, more peering down the rope with my week-old batteries and still no response. I've already worked out the probable cause. I remember the back-and-forth swing at the bottom of the pitch created by the force of the waterfall; the swinging of the rope must have hooked a flake on the unstable wall below the anchor and sent it down onto Dave.

It's hard to decide what to do; the weight of Dave's body and probably some of the packs, hangs on the rope, making descent difficult. Should I try and haul him up? Is the anchor strong enough for that? Am I? Is he even alive? I hang in the dark, trying to think through the enormity of what has just happened.

I shout some more into the darkness, and eventually Dave groans in response to my questions: 'You alright?', 'Can you climb up? More groaning. The feeling of dread begins to lift; we can get out of this.

Dave starts climbing. When he finally crawls into the field of my light he is quite a sight. His helmet is cleaved in two and hangs preposterously around his neck by the chinstrap. His headlamps have been torn off. His face and overalls are shredded, exposing a battered-looking shoulder; there is loads of blood.

Patching up ensues at the top of the fourth pitch, before we continue slowly up, our packs getting heavier all the time as we ascend the remaining pitches and de-rig them behind us. I do lots of double trips as Dave lies down to recover, but as we progress he seems to perk up and is able to haul the packs like a one-armed seaman. At the bottom of the exit pitch I have a strong sense of déjà vu watching Dave slowly climb the rope, again in a steaming shaft of blue light, again slowly, slowly, to the outside world.

We emerge to a foot of new snow on the ground, and observing the sky turning red in the east, we congratulate ourselves on exiting the cave at sunrise, except that it then proceeds to get dark. We don't realise, at this stage, that we have spent nine days in the cave. We sit there on the small mountain of our packs, slowly beginning to freeze in our wet clothes. The new snow will make the already difficult job of moving our gear even more treacherous and unpleasant. We are absolutely spent and can do no more than find and hunker down in our damp sleeping bags. But when I look at Dave in the dying light of my torch I see, beneath the mud and the blood and the tears, the glimmer of a goofy smile and I have to laugh too. Somehow, through it all, something in what we've done is just what we came for.

A river with Dave

After this, Dave and I went back to rafting, perhaps deciding that you had to draw the line somewhere. We never returned to caving; rivers certainly seemed a lot cleaner. Dave, keen to extend his do-it-yourself philosophy to rafting, was disappointed to discover that it had all been done before. The basic outline of a raft made from tyre tubes was described in an entertaining book called *Wild Rivers*, which also recounted the early descents of several classic rivers during the 1970s. The 'single man' design we ended up adopting and perfecting was based on one in the book.

The process of construction would begin by finding old tubes at a garage and repairing them. Two truck tubes, end on end, were lashed to a manuka pole underneath, and a smaller stick across the front for a footrest. Packs went in the rear tube, upright for a backrest. Paddle blades were pre-cut from ply and attached to suitable sticks from the forest when we arrived at the get-in. We carried a bike pump and repair patches. This make-it-on-the-spot approach meant that we could carry all the ingredients into remote locations, build a raft and then go rafting. The trip in *Wild Rivers* that most grabbed our attention was, of course, the gnarliest, and also the one we decided to do first – the Karamea.

Like most adventures with Dave, this one started with loading up the buggy with lots of gear and dressing warmly. This time, the trip north was extra demanding in temperature terms, requiring that we wear most of our clothes and even our sleeping bags. It started snowing somewhere up the Waiau Valley and by the time we were approaching the Lewis Pass, it was dark and snow was falling in big fat flakes. Dave was having trouble with visibility as the snow goggles he wore for driving were riming over. I was huddled in my sleeping bag covered in snow and the two-wheel-drive buggy was starting to lose traction when a building loomed out of the darkness. It turned out to be a gravel shed which, being dry and roofed, was a substantial comfort upgrade. We spent the night there dossed in the gravel.

There was still snow on the tops by the time we made it into Karamea Bend some two days later, and the weather had cleared to a crisp, fine spell of autumn weather. After a long walk down the Leslie River we were happy to dump our heavy packs. And it's always good to arrive at the start of something: the bottom of a mountain, the mouth of a cave, the headwaters of a river.

There is an added excitement too, in wilderness, and the Karamea certainly seemed wild. Once we started on the river at the Bend, we would be committed. The area downstream is a gazetted wilderness zone and there is little in the way of tracks or easy routes in and out of the area. The river itself we knew little about, apart from the descriptions in *Wild Rivers* of tumultuous rapids, clouds of voracious sandflies and spooky lakes full of eels. The lakes were the result of the 1929 Murchison earthquake, which had sent mountainsides of debris down into the river valley and dammed the flow of the river; years later, they are still there. Far above the river, on the true left, the valley walls are capped by the spectacular scarp of the Garibaldi Range, a marbleised cliff-line overlying a deeper band of granite, large pieces of which now lay along our route, apparently blocking the flow of the river in the form of rapids a kilometre long. We had never heard of such a thing; we had a lot to learn.

The first thing that struck me on getting into the water was how cold it was, and it was made even chillier by the skimpiness and shortness of my wetsuit. Dave, for once, wasn't the one doing it the hardest, having brought along a full-length dive suit. Within a few minutes of getting wet, my feet went numb and pretty much stayed that way for the duration. For the next four days, I was never warm.

The first day, as we came to grips with the new (to us) techniques of river-running, we discovered it meant a lot more swimming than we had imagined, especially early on. We found that the raft design was relatively nimble and good for avoiding obstacles, but not so good for punching through turbulence. Because of the weight of the packs on the back, the boats had a habit of flipping over backwards up the face of big waves, which meant an ignominious exit for us over the rear, followed by frantic manoeuvres to get back on. We shot the lower half of many rapids just by clinging on in any way we could. The rapids and scenery were magnificent, but as the day wore on, I got colder and colder. We lost our paddles after a particularly gruelling swim and had to make some more. It got dark again as we paddled into the head of the biggest of the earthquake lakes, and then it just got darker.

Cold and tired and probably a tad hypothermic, I remember little until coming to while following Dave through the bush in the dark. Once I got around to asking, I was told we were looking for a hut – specifically the Roaring Lion Hut – and apparently we were lost. We had left our rafts in the bush somewhere down the way and the hut was up ahead somewhere. For what seemed like an age I stumbled around after Dave until eventually we smelt woodsmoke, followed our noses and soon after found the hut. I vaguely recall being fed fresh trout and potatoes and looked after by friendly fishermen before falling asleep, heavily. By the next morning, though, I had managed to regain my bearings, humour and appetite. We sat outside the hut and ate another big feed of fish and spuds before wandering in the sunshine down to our rafts, and a day of what turned out to be even higher drama.

From the lake above it, the outlet rapid to the Roaring Lion lake has a certain presence: a straight across 'horizon' line, beyond which lies a tumble of enormous boulders, a constant hanging cloud of spray and a deep, ominous rumble. We beached onto the first of the landslide rocks and went to investigate. As far as we knew, no one had ever run this rapid and, even to us, it seemed obvious enough why. The first series of chutes and drops all piled into a house-sized boulder about 100 metres down and most of the river seemed to disappear under it, before frothing up on the downstream side and carrying on in a series of crazy cascades for as far as we could see.

We untied our packs from the rafts and shouldered them. Scrambling over and among the boulders alongside the rapid, it seemed to take an age before we arrived at the bottom of the rapid and ditched them. The trouble started as we walked back up to collect the rafts.

'That bit there looks doable,' said Dave.

He was right – it did. So did the next bit. The problem was, every section that looked doable seemed to end in a bit that looked undoable. Usually, this meant where the bulk of the river went under a huge rock.

'Be alright without the packs, I reckon.'

Dave had a point there too: without the weight of the packs the rafts would be much more manoeuvrable and that would be vital for choosing the best route through the maze of boulders.

'Okay, we'll just do it in sections then,' Dave decided.

The problem of the unrunnable rapid was now resolved: we would just hop in and run the 'doable' bits, without packs. On our way back up to the top of the rapid, we carefully scouted out the route and tried to keep the more obvious landmarks in our minds. It looked outrageous but I supposed we hadn't come here not to go rafting.

Once we were down on the river at water level, our perspective seemed very different and our carefully memorised lines were quickly lost in the confusing scale of the boulder field. So it was, that somewhere around the Big Red Rock, where we had determined that we should go right, Dave went left. Or, equally likely, I shouted out that we were supposed to go left when in fact we should have gone right. The outcome was the same: we went, inevitably, the wrong way, and from my vantage point a few metres behind Dave, he disappeared disturbingly quickly. I, as one does in these situations, followed him without thinking. From the lip of the drop, there was a worrying, if brief, view of things. The waterfall dropped some 3 metres into a narrow foaming pool. Dave had washed up into a tiny and shallow eddy off to the side and I seemed to read, in the brief moment before I too fell off the waterfall, a sort of 'Nooo, don't come this way' look in his eyes.

I landed violently in the foam at the bottom and, in the ensuing turmoil, had the overwhelming urge to no longer be in this river, so was mightily relieved to be quite quickly washed up onto a protruding slab of rock. We crawled far enough away from the noise of the river for the rock to be dry, and lay there, savouring our survival. Apart from the odd groan from Dave, nothing was said for a while until he announced, and it was almost as if I'd expected it, that he thought he'd broken his leg. 'It was that rock I landed on. Didn't you land on it too?'

I looked at his leg. Under the thickness of the wetsuit it did indeed seem deformed, as if a large bite had been taken out of the shin. He looked very pale. I gazed at the waterfall and where it landed on the rock; that I had somehow missed it seemed inconceivable, as did the fact that my legs were intact. I climbed up onto a higher rock to regain some perspective. It was at this exact moment that a helicopter flew up the rapid at low level, and it felt, very briefly, as if there was a moment in time, a portal to another potential reality, right there to be taken, and then it was past. The pilot briefly saw us over his shoulder but didn't come back to check.

I went off downstream to collect our rafts from various nooks and crannies and when I returned, Dave was looking somewhat perkier: 'Don't think it's broken after all.' This didn't surprise me either – as if a mere waterfall and a big chunk of limestone would be enough to set Dave back for long. I was relieved, though; the disappearing helicopter had reminded me how very much we were on our own.

We were reunited with our gear at the bottom of the rapid, after hauling our rafts over the rocks for the remaining distance. The section we had completed was only a small segment of the entire rapid and, thanks to our recent experience, we realised how optimistic our ambitions had been. Dave was limping heavily but seemed to think that his leg would be just fine for rafting. I had no reason to expect that it wouldn't be. 'That'll be the worst of it,' he said. I supposed so too, but neither of us really knew.

For the next two days there was indeed nothing worse. Travel down the river was, in fact, magnificent. The weather held fine and the setting, below the dramatic escarpment of the Garibaldi and the deep green forest, was spectacular. The water seemed full of life in the form of eels and trout and in the quieter sections there was always birdsong. The river fell in a continuous series of pools and drops and, although beautiful, was constantly challenging. Spills were commonplace, but as the river gained in size the swims seemed to become cleaner, with fewer of the chaotic rock jumbles of the earthquake dams. Falling in was still a cold prospect, however, and happened often enough. We took the hint, rafting through the sunny hours of the day, and stopping early to light big fires to warm ourselves. We woke every morning covered in frost.

So it was that, on the evening of our third day on the river, with the sky growing dark with cloud and evening coming on, we arrived at Greys Hut. Situated in a small clearing just before the river constricts into the lower gorge, Greys was an old and seldom used shelter, tenuously connected to the outside world via a long day of tramping along the gorge track. My favourite entry in the hut book came from 15 years before: 'Crashed the chopper in the creek yesterday. Walking out tomorrow.'

The greatest bounty in the hut, though, I found under one of the bunks: a pile of old woolly long-johns – the old pink one-piece Farmer John style with button-up flaps and smelling only faintly of mouse poo. Two layers of these under my wetsuit would put an end to my cold problems. The next morning I set off looking like some kind of West Coast hillbilly superhero, but from then on I stayed warm.

It rained heavily all night and in the morning the river was running high and a little discoloured. There was talk of using the track to walk out, but we resolved to give the river a go; we could always bail out if we had to. Decision-making like this is often an exercise in talking about things you really know nothing about. All we knew of the Karamea Gorge was that it contained big rapids and people had done them and survived.

There was an ominous feeling to the day, though, as we pushed into the flow and flounced onto our rafts. Downstream, the walls of the valley quickly narrowed and we could hear the deep rumble of rapids before we could see them. We pulled out of the river just before it disappeared, obviously, into the gorge. Standing on a large rock that protruded into the flow, we eyed up the first rapid, which looked particularly unappealing. From where we were, the river ran swiftly towards a vertical bluff, into which it ploughed full steam before staging a 90-degree turn to the left and disappearing from sight. An eddy that more resembled a giant cartoon whirlpool circulated evilly on the inside

of the corner, rising and then falling to well below the level of the water
around it, a kind of suck-hole to nowhere.

Dave took the initiative. 'We'll throw a stick in and see what happens.'

The stick disappeared into the rapid. We didn't see it again.

'Too small to see,' Dave theorised.

A series of larger sticks, culminating in a ponderous two-person log,
were tossed into the entry to the rapid. We never saw any of them again.

'They must've made it through then,' Dave decided and as if to
prove him right, a blue duck sailed proudly down past us, crested the
massive buffer wave at the bluff, hovering there perilously for a moment
before coolly riding off downstream, also never to be seen again. This
galvanised us into action: having been shown the line, we slipped past
the hole and into the gorge.

The Karamea Gorge was, in every way, huge – the size of the waves,
the rapids themselves, the walls above us. We stopped where we could
to scout upcoming difficult sections with a rough rule of thumb: if
we could see the exit to the rapid from the approach, we would run it
without scouting, and if we couldn't see the end, which usually meant
it was an extra steep rapid, then we would get out and have a look. This
seemed good in theory, but several times we left it too late to decide
before being committed. It was absolutely thrilling.

At one stage my raft, with pack, became pinned on a log halfway
down a drop, catapulting me off the front and necessitating an arduous
team effort to extract it. We were able to climb under the drop itself
and heave like bulls until something gave way and freed the raft back
into the current. I then had to dive in to hang onto it all the way
down the rapid. The succession of rapids, the pools between them
only brief enough to catch your breath in, was relentless. I remember
careering down a section of giant waves, screaming in excitement.
Slowly the pace of the river slackens and the valley walls angle back.
Just as there's an excitement in arriving somewhere, equally there's a
satisfaction in coming to the end, and having done so well. We wind
down along with the energy of the river, gradually and naturally.

The last couple of hours are spent paddling hard into the sea breeze that had risen, seemingly just to draw out the process of finishing up. Finally, bush gives way to paddocks and we arrive at the road bridge. We get stiffly off our boats, happy to have stopped paddling, hungry but also reluctant to part with the river.

From here it will be a long hitchhike back to the buggy at the Flora Saddle carpark. We look at our trusty rafts and decide to leave them where they are, as is, for whoever wants them. The woman who picks us up reckons they'll be great for the kids; funny how I feel sentimental about not seeing them again.

We spend that night under a gigantic old pear tree at Inangahua Junction. (The pears were delicious and years later, the tree is still there). Dave and I part ways temporarily at the Murchison turn-off, as Dave heads off to retrieve the buggy. Rather than hitch on in the rain, I hole up under the O'Sullivans Bridge over the Buller, waiting for Dave to come by and pick me up on the way back to Christchurch. It's the next day before he does but that's okay; having slept the night by a river again, I hardly want to go home anyway.

Travelling in the buggy now seems less of an adventure than it was; the road beneath us is smooth and unmoving, the views are more of people and their works, and even the cold whistling around us is no longer a novelty. Sitting side by side, we make plans for the next mission. Dave starts listing other rivers to be done, and do them we will, but as I look up past the valley walls, the snow-covered mountain tops are picked out sharply against the blue of the afternoon sky. In the clear air they look close, but also far away. There is nothing to be heard over the muttering of the engine and the wind whistling in our ears, except, perhaps, for the mountains calling my name.

PART TWO

GREYWACKE

Go to any beach in Aotearoa, pick up the wet sand and squeeze it into a ball in your fist. Imagine burying the ball so that, over time, pressured by their own weight, the grains pack tightly into something harder, until it holds together and becomes rock. This is greywacke, made from the detritus of the land, washed into the sea, buried and then risen from oceanic depths.

To a climber, one of the chief attributes of greywacke is its variability. Fractured and pulverised, or weathered and solid, greywacke comes from the same source, but manifests differently. It can form into the Weet-Bix of the Main Divide – fearful stacks of tottering instability – or the hard boulders of Baring Head, washed smooth by the waves. In New Zealand it's everywhere, and makes up the building blocks of much of the Southern Alps/Kā Tiritiri o te Moana. Although only occasionally reliable, it always makes the best scree slopes to run down.

There are some firmer outcrops of this essential rock here and there. When climbing, this is what you look for and, luckily, some of the upthrust buttresses of our highest peaks are reasonably solid. The best greywacke carries a roughened red exterior, the worst comes in the colours of an old bruise. It is often the first rock mountaineers encounter, and as a climber, I grew to both love and hate it. To start with though, greywacke was something of a gateway drug and I didn't care that it was unreliable. The mountains made of it were big and spectacular and, in the beginning, that was all I was looking for.

Don't tell mum

Mountaineering seemed a somehow nobler calling than floating down rivers on tyre tubes and grovelling through narrow caves, despite its well known hazards, and in the early 1980s, I ended up in the Canterbury University Tramping Club. I was in the right place – the CUTC was brimming with enthusiastic neophytes. The main protagonists were, mostly, hairy. Huge bushy beards, unruly hair and an unkempt demeanour were the look of the era. These people seemed to me wildly mountainous, and extremely experienced. Some had even climbed large snowy peaks in the Southern Alps, like Mount Tasman.

A story that impressed me initially concerned an ascent of the Heemskirk Face of Tasman, in winter. The boys (we shall call them), having skinned up from Pioneer Hut in deep snow, left their skis at the bottom of the route and waded for several hours up the steep snow slope that is most of the face. Upon arriving at the icy headwall one of them, to get established before roping up, plunged his ice axe shaft into the soft snow. From this tiny trigger point the entire face they had just ascended avalanched, leaving the four of them – miraculously – not swept away. The only thing they could do was feel lucky as they watched their skis disappear under hundreds of tonnes of debris. After descending, they spent 12 days stuck in the hut for the duration of a storm. This story just proved to me how experienced these university types were and I became determined to get involved. So it was, that the first life-threatening mountain experiences of mine came early in my alpine climbing career.

❖

The keen hairy type I spent most of my climbing time with was Hans. He seemed worldly wise and knowledgeable; thinking back, I guess he was about 20. Anyway, he had a big beard and I could barely manage a bit of patchy bum fluff.

The prevailing wisdom among the climber types in the club, was that winter was the time to go climbing in the mountains because it was 'more technical'. I didn't really know what this meant, but it sounded good to me, so I invested in some second-hand gear and put my hand up. We usually ended up at Arthur's Pass, where the mountains of the Main Divide are both spectacular and accessible. A look at accident statistics shows that the highest number of accidents occur on the more accessible peaks.

Because I was so inexperienced, Hans thought we should do something easy for a first climb, and chose the South Face of Mount Phipps, across from the Temple Basin ski field. It was the depths of winter. We started up the middle of the face, to the right of some large bluffs, before angling back leftwards above them. The snow was soft and deep, and it took some time wading steeply through it to get to the trickier-looking section higher up, where a steeper cliff-band was coated in something more like ice.

We stopped at the base of this section and Hans set about constructing an anchor, since I had no real idea of how to do so in the unconsolidated powder. As it turned out, Hans didn't either. After tying me in and getting the ropes sorted, he set off, directly up to a steep band of ice, which looked intimidating, mainly because ice climbing was also something I didn't know much about.

Hans started scratching tenuously up the icy wall and, with my bendy tramping boots and old-school crampons, things weren't looking too flash. Not to worry, though, I'd have a rope from above and Hans was onto it. The ice was brittle and variable and the climbing looked insecure. After a few minutes he stopped and placed an ice screw for protection, before continuing. To me it looked unlikely that the screw

would hold a fall, but what did I know? Hans continued, hacking his
way up the wall. Fragments of ice rattled down the face and then,
all of a sudden, so did Hans.

When he came off, he was some 20 metres directly above me.
The runner he'd placed didn't hold. I had time enough to register what
was happening and start frantically hauling in rope before Hans landed
heavily, yet surprisingly quietly, in the snow next to me. I had to jump
aside so he didn't land *on* me. Unfortunately, he didn't stop there, but
carried on at high speed towards the bluffs below. I braced myself on
my stance, readying for the expected force as the rope pulled tight but
it never did – the soft snow anchor didn't even begin to hold the force
of the fall and I was plucked straight off. In the next second we were
both hurtling together through the deep snow towards the cliff below,
connected by a now worthless rope.

We stopped before the impending bluffs, about 20 metres below
our original stance – grinding to a halt in the deep snow. Both of us
were completely unscathed. I don't really remember how we reacted
or the discussion we had, but I do seem to recall that the flavour of it
was one of humour. I guess surviving makes you happy. We must have
felt okay because we regrouped and carried on to the top, taking an
easier line. This episode, especially because it was my first 'technical'
outing, gained some notoriety in tramping club circles (but I didn't tell
my mum), and I felt that I was really getting some experience. Not long
after, I got a whole lot more.

By this stage I had done some rock climbing, mostly around the
Port Hills. 'Training for the greater ranges' was only somewhat tongue-
in-cheek in 1982 and I was burning to lead something in the mountains.
Hans and I, having learnt our lesson, decided on something bigger for
our next outing, which happened to fall over the winter solstice. The
Otira Face of Rolleston was something of a test-piece in the club at the

time and seemed just the thing. I knew nothing about it; I just said yes.

The weekend was one of blue skies, settled weather and deep winter cold – 14° below zero in Arthur's Pass village on the night of our adventure, one of the coldest temperatures ever recorded there. Apart from being pretty much the chilliest time of the year, the reduced daylight hours meant the day's climbing would feel really short. More significantly, the night would end up being really long. Hans, who in his extensive career as an alpinist had suffered a fair bit of discomfort, had the foresight to bring along some 'just in case' gear in the form of a two-person nylon bivvy bag and a cooker. No food, really, just something to get us through a night of potential deprivation.

My memories of the day are a bit hazy – concussion will do that. We must have got off to a cracking early start because we ended up quite high on the face by around lunchtime. I remember thinking that the climbing was fabulous. It seemed like the real thing at last: putting in gear, clipping the rope, belaying – all the stuff I'd been hankering for. The route had only a little snow and ice on it and it was mostly rock climbing and not too difficult. Towards the top, the face steepened up for the last few pitches and the climbing became even more like … well, climbing. Hans whacked some pitons in and hung off them – just like the pictures in the *Mountain* magazines we read so avidly in the university library – and then I headed off up a steepish corner feature. I found the pitch absorbing and satisfying; there I was, in the mountains, doing it.

I do have quite a clear vision of the moment it all went wrong; of pulling onto a ledge at the top of the corner, and reaching my fingers into a crack at the back of it. My last memory of any sort, for many hours, was of the ledge shifting towards me as I hauled up onto it, a horrid grating of grit under the slab of rock as it shifted me out into space, and that was it. The next thing for me was the darkness of night, and pain. I was still climbing but everything was different. The rope was above me now and I was in an icy gully. The pain came from trying to kick some purchase into the hard snow of the gully, with a smashed-up ankle. One arm was broken, bound in a makeshift sling, and the other clung to my ice axe, with which I was trying to claw my way up.

It was the agony of the kicking that had woken me up. Without knowing or wondering why, I kept at it, certain that this is what I had to do. I finally arrived where Hans was, a snowy place where a small sharp ridge of snow butted into a rock-band and this was where we made do. I don't remember feeling scared; it was for Hans to make all the decisions that night. We yelled out loudly towards the light of some headlamps we saw descending the standard route of the Otira Slide. We couldn't tell if they'd heard us.

We spent a long time preparing ourselves for the bivvy. The sky was huge and starry until we pulled the bag down over our heads for the night. Then the stars were gone and it was just the closeness of the bag, the frozen condensation and the awkward rustling. The shivering, once it started, was violent and couldn't be stopped.

Hans explained to me what had happened, how he had ducked as the rock I'd pulled off had disintegrated above him, some of the bits destroying his helmet, and how I'd ended up hanging down below him on the rope, broken and delirious. And how, for the rest of the afternoon, we had climbed up to our present position high on the face. We were a long way from the valley floor and, we thought, not far from the summit and the relatively straightforward descent.

To this day I don't know why we didn't retreat after the fall, why we went up and not down, but Hans had his reasons and I still trust that they were good ones. Certainly I was quite functional in some ways. I did manage the couple of pitches we climbed afterwards, although I was apparently behaving like a lunatic most of the time. Hans has several anecdotes regarding my erratic behaviour throughout the afternoon, as he sought to get us out of our predicament. I expounded various far-fetched theories on this and that, spent half an hour trying to remove a five-dollar piton and then refused to retrieve one of his expensive cams. I lost blood, but not, apparently, my sense of humour.

I spent the night swamped in pain and shaking with cold. Hans wrapped me with his body and lit the cooker when the chill became too much. This, and our flimsy layer of nylon, allowed us to make it through the night which, as they do, passed, though ever so slowly. The sun rose directly onto us and we spent some time soaking in its thin warmth, waiting and hoping. Just after we'd decided that no one had heard our cries for help and we'd better get on with rescuing ourselves, we heard the chopper, like a fast and distant heartbeat from the valley.

They found us quickly. The pilot hovered with a skid off the end of the arête we were camped on; a gut-wrenching and wobbly step and we were back into a world where other people would look after us. To this day, the sound of an air force Iroquois lifts my heart. And announces an epic.

This story also had its humorous side. The Canterbury volunteer search and rescue team, alerted by the team descending the Slide, were called out for our rescue at the end of a long night of socialising at their annual dinner. Some severely hungover people had to make their way up to a freezing Arthur's Pass at a very early hour to come and get us. This was worth a few beers to us and, in the natural way of things, everyone was pleased with the outcome. There was also a less humorous side. On the same day, on Mount Christina in the Darrans, someone else had fallen to their death. From Mount Crosscut, friends of mine had watched the body being flown out below the helicopter. Things can go either way.

It's really interesting to reflect on how I looked at things then, how comprehensively I ignored what didn't suit me. My degree of acceptance that this was just the way things were, that these things just happened in climbing, is retrospectively frightening. I think that death meant absolutely nothing to me. There was just an incredible focus on doing this climbing thing – this thing that I really felt was me. Imagine that: dying before even having an inkling of death, knowing only the grand magnificence of a youthful life.

And maybe all these near misses just made things seem a bit more meaningful. When you're young and you find something that has meaning, you grab it. I wasn't actively looking for meaning, not then, but youth seems to crave experience. This creates memories that one day, if you live long enough, cause you to reflect. The meaning may come, but seldom at the time.

I have in a photo album some low-quality colour prints – the little ones with rounded corners, the ones that go pink with age – that show me getting out of the chopper back at Wigram, looking a bit beaten up and with a wry grin on my face. There's another one taken on the day, of the Otira Face with a dotted squiggly line up the middle, ending in a red x. There's another of Hans on Phipps, just before he fell off.

There was a stint in hospital and a couple of operations. There was media coverage. I was visited by relatives and by my mother who, having waited for something like this to happen for a while, seemed relieved that at least I was alive. I don't think I even considered ceasing to go climbing. Why would I?

I imagine my mother would have worried less had I learnt my craft at a school of mountaineering rather than the school of hard knocks and near misses. It is easy now, or even the accepted way, to pay to learn the necessary skills through a professional organisation. Previously, many of these skills were acquired through a do-it-yourself attitude and/ or the gloriously random and often erratic tutelage of a club. Having been a Girl Guide leader, my mother was into clubs. Had she known a bit more about the ones in which I was involved, she may not have been quite so thrilled.

I moved to Dunedin to finish my degree, but even the few hours a week needed to do this became incompatible with the flexibility required to go climbing when conditions were good, or just whenever I felt like it. The student lifestyle was an entertaining one without the intrusions of actual study, and to help out, there were plenty of outdoors types to get distracted with.

There were a few differences from Canterbury. A drinking culture was even more embedded in the Otago University Tramping Club.

Weekend outings to the hilly regions invariably involved a few hours of driving and ended up with bottles of cheap liquor rolling around the floors of rented vans. The people were different too, but only in the sense that they didn't seem quite so hairy and unkempt, or perhaps there were more women. One thing, though, was much the same – keenness. And if being a student means anything, it means not letting a lack of knowledge, or much else, get in the way of being keen.

August in New Zealand is pretty much the depths of the alpine winter and, potentially, a serious time to go mountaineering. The winter snow lies deep and it's been blown around a lot, making travel more difficult and a high avalanche hazard more likely. The storms can be ferocious and although it's past the solstice, temperatures will be generally low. This creates an ideal set-up for deep-ending a bunch of novice mountaineers on a skills course which, although achieved in an ad hoc and well-meaning way, was the tried and true outcome of the annual OUTC snowcraft trip to Arthur's Pass. There had been various excitements on these courses over the years, and rumour had it that the chief ranger would arrange his annual leave to avoid being there and having to deal with the fallout.

The first set of skills that need to be imparted on any mountaineering course, are the ones promoting survival. Although we did emphasise this aspect – inadvertently perhaps – there was enough luck thrown into the mix that it mostly turned out alright, and humour was a constant presence. My qualifications for being an instructor were pretty impressive – I'd survived Phipps and been rescued off Rolleston – which by default made me one of the more senior tutors. Most of the others were my flatmates or weekend 'mission' companions and their qualifications were generally more modest: they'd mostly done the course as pupils the year before. And, of course, they were keen.

Day one was spent on the learning the basics, like trudging up the Mount Avalanche track with a hangover and cold hands and feet to muck around with the unfamiliar gear of the winter mountaineer: ice axes, snow stakes and so on. A chute was made in the soft snow to allow the students to slide down it at speed, in order to practise self-arresting skills and belaying. Everyone got thoroughly cold and wet and the weather came in, so we retreated early for the obligatory debrief at the Jacksons pub, a half-hour drive away.

There were other hazards besides the climbing and drinking. Van traversing – climbing out one of the side windows, making your way over the roof and back in via the opposite side window – was a good example. According to my 'instructors', this was best practised on slow twisty sections of mountain road such as the Otira zigzag, and best of all at night, on the way back from the pub. Advanced technique required van traversing to be completed in a light snowstorm. It sounds counterintuitive, but such conditions made the tricky moves across the holdless middle section easier, if you timed the corners correctly. Once mastered, it was a thrilling and entertaining way to wash away the worries and stresses accumulated over the days of alpine instruction. At the very least, it added an air of perspective to proceedings, a reminder that life in the mountains had risks that came with the territory.

Those risks were somewhat elevated the next morning. Plenty of new snow had fallen and with it came lots of wind – the sort of conditions that move the snow from windy to sheltered aspects, and deposit even greater amounts on those slopes facing away from the blast. Even we knew that it was a bit hazardous out there. Despite this, three different groups, including mine, decided to attempt Rome Ridge, a fine, snaking ridgeline leading to the top of Mount Rolleston. It was a beautiful day, after all. Before we set off, somewhat delayed thanks to the lingering effects of the pub, another party of three – the course cooks – had set off to also climb Rolleston via the more usual route of the Otira Slide, which intersects with Rome Ridge just below Low Peak.

About an hour's travel above the bushline, the broad shoulder of the ridge flattens off briefly before rising in a short wall and narrowing up considerably. My flatmate Andrew, instructing a couple of the stronger pupils, was in the lead at this point and by the time we arrived, had decided to branch off on another mission entirely – the Crow Face of Rolleston – which required that they cross an adjacent bowl to access their intended climb. I suggested that this seemed an ambitious proposal in the conditions. 'I'll just go for a wee look around the corner, and see what it's like,' said Andrew.

At the same time the other group, led by Paul, decided to carry on up the ridge and since there was room for only one party at a time, my group sat down to wait. Andrew disappeared around the corner, Paul disappeared up the ridge and we ate our sandwiches. Soon, a faint cry came from around the corner. Following Andrew's footsteps, I came upon quite a sight. His pupils were halfway across a wide snow slope, standing there unmoving. From the line of their tracks an avalanche had cut across the entire breadth of the snowfield. Even from 100 metres away it was obvious they were petrified.

I looked around for Andrew, finally spotting him some 200 metres down the slope, where it started to flatten off, on a moving mass of avalanche debris. Rather than be buried deep within the wreckage, he had somehow managed to stay on top and was riding out the last few metres before it all came to a stop. The cry I had heard was him shouting with an adrenalised joy that he was actually going to survive. By the time I'd gone and helped the hapless pupils back across to us, Andrew was starting the long trek back up; a small price to pay, considering.

Paul's group, unaware of any of these events, was preparing to forge on up towards the crest of the ridge – another lee slope. My group, keen to get going, had already started up a gully below them which, I belatedly realised, was directly in the firing line should the slope above them release. I looked around, feeling that things were getting out of control. I shouted to Paul to wait up, told Andrew's team to stay where they were – no argument there – and booted it up to my crew. Charging up in their footsteps, I arrived at the top of the gully breathless and apprehensive that at any stage the slope above might collapse onto us. My pupils arrived and we positioned ourselves on a small knob, out of the way, we hoped, of any avalanche.

A bit closer now, I suggested to Paul that perhaps his group might reconsider continuing. He replied that, because they were well advanced on the slope, they would carry on to the ridge and wait there. One by one, the group above crested the slope onto the ridge until there were only two people left near the top. Our group waited below, my pupils eager to continue, even as I insisted that we stay where we were.

This avalanche was deeper set than the first, breaking off in eerie silence before gathering momentum. It was mesmerising, in a looking-a-snake-in-the-eyes kind of way, as it came towards us, with nowhere else to go. As the mass of snow hit the rise we were on, it parted either side of us before pouring into the gully we had just climbed, and over into the basin below. We stood very still, not moving at all until the noise of the debris grinding to a halt below had subsided. It had been a close call.

Above us, one of the students was pinned immobile to the slope and it seemed obvious that this moment was the end of her alpine climbing career. Directly above her, standing on a slab of snow that had not yet slid off, was Paul. 'Shall I knock this bit off too?' he shouted down, before coming to his senses. The hazard now reduced, I climbed up the slope to take a look along the next section of the ridge. Cornices hung over the sharper parts and the slopes below them were pregnant with snow. It was obviously hazardous. There was no question of continuing, so we all made our careful way back down.

We regrouped at the base of the steep bit, nobody looking quite as keen as before. Andrew had come down from his survival high. The usual 'whatever doesn't kill you' remarks were made, jokes were cracked. Andrew told us how the second avalanche had nearly taken him out; he'd had to run away from it and then ascend the snow slope for a second time. My group were quite impressed with my parting of the waters trick; I was thankful for the good luck involved. We sat, newly appreciative of the beauty of our surroundings, before descending to the hut for a well-earned early dinner.

Dinner didn't really happen. The cooks weren't back from their climb of Rolleston. Several of the other parties had also had their adventures in the snow and it was during one of these catch-up conversations that someone said, 'Did you see those guys on Rome Ridge?'

'Er, what guys?'

'The cooks – they were going to descend that way.'

There was a collective putting of things together in our minds: the lateness of the hour, the relative inexperience of the cooks' party, the way the ridge had looked from our high point. It seemed that the day was not yet over.

Labouring back up the ridge, we met up with them just after midnight, an hour or so above the bushline, with the weather starting to pack in again. They were tired but still going, and had an epic tale. They had climbed the Low Peak of Rolleston and then descended Rome Ridge, mostly in the dark. One of them, on one of her first ever alpine outings, had saved another climber from a fall to certain doom. She had managed this feat on a shaft belay, where an ice axe is shoved in the snow behind your foot and the rope braked by wrapping it around your ankle – a very old-school technique that in reality seldom works. It was the first time she'd ever used one.

On the slow descent, one of the cooks asked to stop for a pee as we stood around in the snow, trying not to fall asleep in our tracks. Nothing much seemed to be happening until he finally said, 'I'm done – let's go.' It didn't strike me as odd, until I watched him emptying his boot out later. It had been a big day all round.

Aoraki

After the beginning of the world, the children of Rakinui, the sky father, came down from their home in the heavens to visit his new wife, Papatūānuku, the earth mother, and to explore the world they had never seen. Aoraki, the first-born, and his brothers travelled extensively across what was then mostly ocean in a magnificent waka – *Te Waka o Aoraki*. When they did not find the land they sought, Aoraki called out the karakia, the incantation, that would raise them back into the heavens, but his incorrect recitation caused the waka to fall back into the sea, there to be stranded on a rock, leaving Aoraki and his brothers marooned, clinging to the hull of the upturned waka. A long time passed and they slowly became stone, their hair turned white and they became the highest peaks of Kā Tiritiri o te Moana – the Southern Alps. They can be seen to this day rising into the sky, Aoraki the highest, their heights cloaked in snow and ice, their physical presence a direct link between tangata whenua – the first people of the land – and their celestial ancestors.

Such is one of the creation stories of Kāi Tahu, the prominent iwi in the South Island, Te Wai Pounamu and it points to the importance of the highest peaks to them. This importance is recognised in several ways, but especially so in the personification of the highest peak, (named Mount Cook by European visitors) as the stony body of Aoraki. Aoraki is also a meaningful landmark for a smaller and more esoteric group of people – mountaineers – but there is a tension. For Māori, no part of a person's body is regarded as more tapu, more sacred, than the head, which makes climbing to the top – to the very head – of the most sacred ancestor of Kāi Tahu something of a dilemma for a mountaineer.

I didn't know that when I was climbing there. I was young and keen and all I knew was that I was continually drawn to the slopes and features of a glorious peak, an ardent moth to a bonfire of hopes and dreams, and probably vanities too. Over several years in the 1980s, me in my early twenties, Aoraki as ageless as ever, I traversed the mountain and climbed most of its aspects, with different companions, on rock and ice, in winter and summer, by established routes and new ones. The mountain and others nearby became the focus of my passions; I was often there in my thoughts. I went there whenever I could and I learnt, among other things, that you had to work really hard to succeed there and that you should go only when the time was right. It was a place I came to know well and it fulfilled me physically and spiritually – those high frozen ridges, those lordly views. All I can think, now, is that there are different ways to revere a mountain, and many ways to show respect, the very least of which would be to forgo standing on the summit.

As time went by, I felt more attuned to Aoraki – the obvious glories, the subtle changes and sudden violence, perhaps a sense of his mana – but I never felt totally at home there. It's only in retrospect, and with the perspective of having climbed elsewhere, that I came to realise why: climbing here is more dangerous than anywhere else in the country.

Vicious, changeable weather and rapidly changing conditions, crevasse-filled glaciers, generally poor rock and narrow valleys lined with unstable seracs, are the features of our highest peaks. If you get through this training ground alive, you're well set up for tackling the greater ranges anywhere – the 'real mountains' that you imagine exist only overseas. The trick to long-term survival is to move on, to where the rock is better, the approaches less threatened, the objective hazard level more reasonable. The West Coast névés, the Aspiring region, the Darrans – anywhere but New Zealand's very highest peaks – are all reasonable options.

But you have only to see what every tourist sees through the bus window on a fine day from the end of Lake Pukaki, to want to go to him. Seen in the flame of sunrise or sunset across the other-worldly blue of the lake, Aoraki is, by any measure, a real mountain. Or a dream.

On my first trip there, with the equally novice Robbo, we walked up Haupapa/Tasman Glacier as far as we could on the awkward rock-covered moraine, avoiding the white ice because we assumed it would be more difficult travel. On our attempt on the Minarets, a moderate snow climb, we were pinned down and then blown over by gale-force winds on hard ice a couple of hours above the hut, before limping our way back down. We then spent some time trapped in the hut in a storm and after walking out in borrowed boots, I contracted a hideous set of infected blisters and a bad case of jock itch. Although we managed to work out on the return trip that it was much easier walking on the white ice, there was still a lot to learn. On my next trip, I climbed Aoraki.

Neither Carol nor I told each other we'd never climbed any of the '10,000-ers' before – the usual prerequisite for tackling Aoraki – and neither did we ask. It just didn't occur to us; we were both burning for the same thing, so off we went, to this real mountain of our dreams. I didn't just want to climb the mountain, however; not for the last time it would be, powerfully and inexplicably, a *feature* that really called to me. The East Ridge of Aoraki rises from the glacial expanse of the Grand Plateau and with nearly 2000 metres of height gain from bottom to top, is one of the proudest and highest features in the land – a mighty journey of classic alpinism. I had seen the ridge on my one visit to the area and immediately it was all I wanted to climb.

We belayed each other across the 'schrund guarding the start of the ridge in the dark of pre-dawn. The blackness below us fell into unimaginable depths and the horror of falling in there was all too obvious. Crossing the frozen bridge that spanned the hole and imagining it collapsing, I realised that there was a finely balanced element of luck – pure and simple blind luck – in what we were doing. We could place good solid anchors in the snow, we could use the right rope techniques, we could do everything correctly, but if the bridge failed at just the wrong moment, then it would be a very ugly situation. We carried on, of course. This is what an alpine life becomes – a life of dilemmas overruled, and then forgotten.

Once we were above the crevasse, the East Ridge rose above us in icy glory, sharpening in the coming light to reveal something far more sizeable than anything I'd encountered before. It felt like a big step up. The ridge at its zenith merges into the summit ridge of Aoraki, the lifted blade of wind-sculpted ice that looks down on everything around it. From the top of the ridge, we would carry on over the Middle Peak, along the 'highest mile', over the summit and down the standard

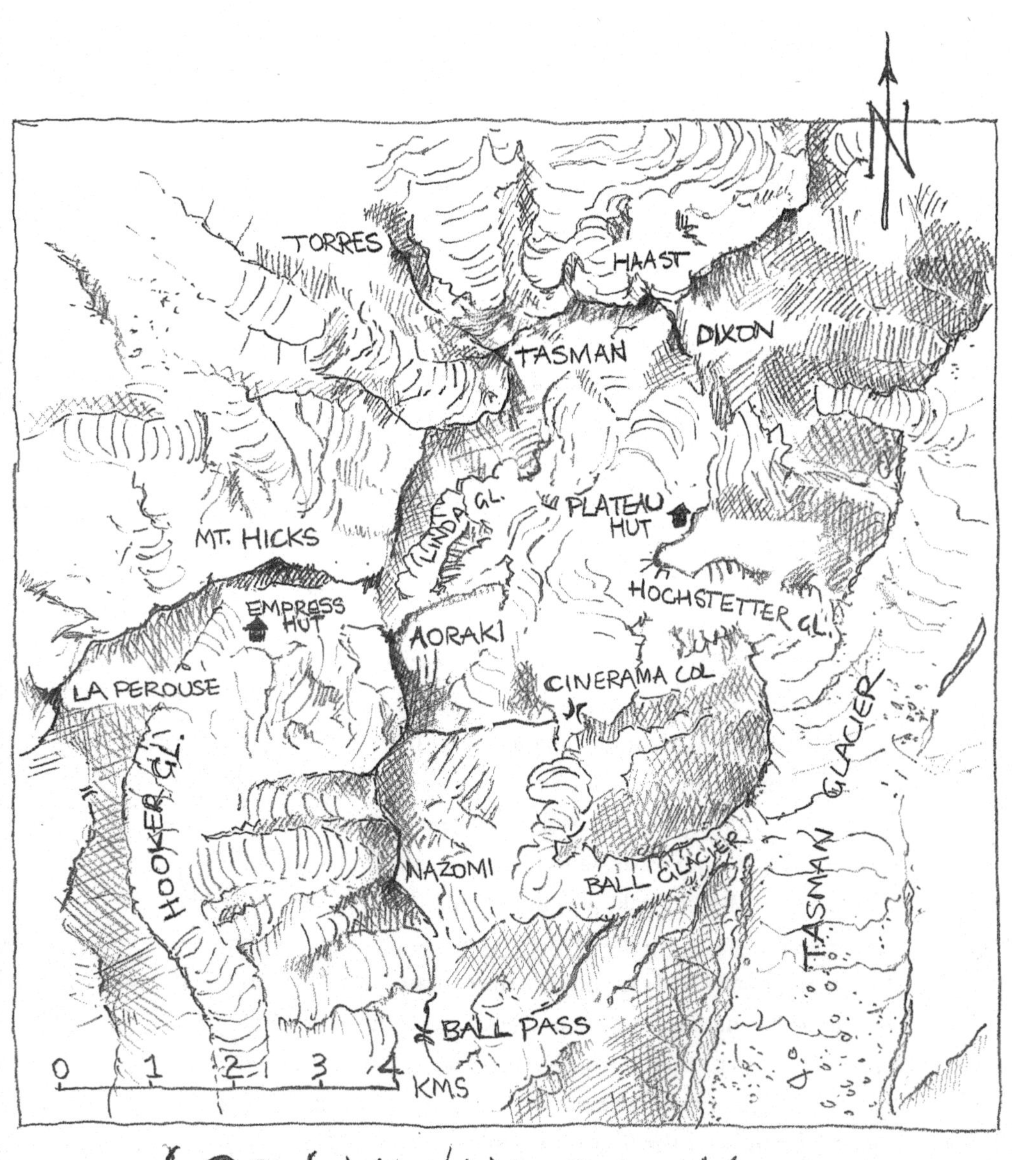

AORAKI / M⁺ COOK

ascent route that follows the Linda Glacier. The route commonly takes a full day to complete, from the obligatory 1 a.m. start right through to the after-dark stumble back into the hut. Sometimes living the dream requires a bit of effort.

There is a section on the East Ridge that is commonly referred to as the 'flat bit' which, although horizontal, is a knife-edge ridge of snow. The standard way to traverse this is to crab along the side wall, stabbing your ice axe into the top of the ridge as you progress. Carol leads confidently across in this style and sets the belay anchor at the far end.

The other, and infinitely more stylish, way to progress across a knife-edge is to stand right on the crest of the ridge and balance precariously across, arms outstretched. Having the rope above me emboldens me to try this and I find it absolutely thrilling, a first taste of big mountain exposure. The dark maw of a crevasse in the dark is forgotten, dispelled by the light, the heights around us and the falling away below us; the position of being halfway to the sky.

The top half of the ridge is a continuous sweep of snow jutting out from the immensity of the faces on either side. Although technically easy, it's a relentless and unforgiving grind. Towards the top, the snow changes to increasingly harder ice, the result of constant polishing by the unrestricted prowling of the westerly winds. We tire and slow, the altitude affecting us too, and the rope is needed again for the final section to the Middle Peak. We cut out small stances in the ice, place ice screws to secure ourselves to the mountain and run out the rope. There's nothing to be heard but the immediate sounds we create: the tinkling of ice shards, the thud of a boot kicked into the ice, harsh breathing. Perhaps there's a backdrop of sound from the now distant valleys – a hush of river-whisper or the breath of wind – perhaps not. There is, though, for the first time, a sense of removal, of being beyond the world. Perhaps this is part of the dream.

Carol is leading, a long way above me as I stand on the belay stance tied into my ice screws, a small step carved out of the ridge crest. The hard ice above requires her to chip away at it with her ice picks

and the fragments clatter down past me, the ridge shedding them off
to the side, disappearing into a greater whiteness on their journey to
the glacier far below. Mesmerised, I follow them with my eyes. We have
been constantly in the sun since it rose, fully in the glare off the frozen
surface we traverse, and have been working hard. The concentration
and effort have been intense and continuous. I close my eyes and lean
back on the rope to relax; then I am falling. A huge surge of adrenaline
snaps me back to attention: I'm hanging on the rope a metre below,
having fallen asleep and slipped off the belay stance. I haven't pulled
Carol off and neither has she noticed. Heart thumping hard, I resolve to
tie myself more tightly into the anchors in future.

The next rope length takes us to the summit ridge and everything
changes. So different this first time – so high, so far above, so beautiful
and consequential, so different from the world we have known before.
It's hard to know what to make of 'getting to the top'. A summit
supposes so much – a fulfilling of purpose, a resolution – and for this
first time, at least, that is indeed how it felt. There is, without doubt, a
sense of exultation and it's a particularly human impulse to stand on top
of something. You know though, even as you do it, that it's a brief and
petty vanity. I doubt that anyone, once they looked around, really felt
that they'd conquered a mountain, especially with the descent still to
come. The top of a mountain is, perhaps, no more than this: the moment
between the end of something and the beginning of something else.

We returned to the hut soon after dark, having completed the climb
in a time of 19 hours – the sort of thing you remember when you're
young and keen – and we were happy with that. I would traverse the
summit ridge of Aoraki several more times over the next few years,
and there would never be any wondering why. That wouldn't happen
for a long time. Carol and I never talked much about her uncertainties
and only a little about the memories she had of her first big mountain.
We did laugh together about hiding our inexperience from each other
beforehand, but I'm not sure that I ever 'fessed up to falling asleep
on the belay. Carol went on to a full and high-achieving life, both in

the mountains and elsewhere. Many years later she was killed in an avalanche while ski-touring in the French Alps, in those real mountains of overseas. I hadn't seen her for a long while and it seemed a distant event, but I still remember that climb: Carol, Aoraki and me.

The first example of what bad weather in the big mountains means to an alpinist, came pretty early for me, in 1985. The standard route up Tasman from the east is the Silberhorn Arête, a classic sweep of snow and ice that rises from the Grand Plateau to join the Main Divide just south of the summit. After that, the sharp blade of the South Ridge is a fitting finish to a mountain which, more than any other in the country, is renowned as an ice peak. Along to the north of the summit, the Syme Ridge drops from the North Shoulder back down in a lovely symmetry to the plateau, a kind of sister route to the Silberhorn. Steve and I planned to ascend the Silberhorn and descend the Syme, a relatively common perambulation of classic ice work; a standard big day out.

We crest the Main Divide about 8 a.m. The view to the west confirms the forecast – there's nothing to worry about in the weather department. A keen breeze from the south-west stings cold on our faces but there's no high cloud or indeed much cloud at all – just an unusual spiral pattern of mist down low and out over the ocean, strangely like a satellite picture of a mini cyclonic feature. We're making good time and there's an exhilaration in being so high so early, with the day stretching out in front of us.

From our position on the Main Divide the last section, the South Ridge, looks absolutely fantastic, the crisp golden light of the eastern side split from the blue shade of the west. We climb in the sunlight, enjoying the secure conditions underfoot that allow us to move freely and confidently, without the distraction of using the rope. As we ascend I notice a hogsback forming over the summit of Aoraki behind us, the thin lenticular cloud a harbinger of wind and possibly storm, but because the sky is still so clear, I don't feel it has any immediate relevance to us. And besides, we're about to summit a beautiful mountain.

As we arrive onto the apex of Tasman some 45 minutes later, a similar cloud starts to form over us too, as if an invisible weight of weather is lowering itself onto the highest summits. We continue over the top with only a brief pause and climb down as the wind picks up and the cloud gathers more thickly around us. As we descend, the cloud base descends with us and for a while we can see that below us the sun is still out. Within the space of 20 minutes, though, we lose any views and by the time we make it to the North Shoulder, visibility is down to a few metres, the wind is howling and we're in a full-on blizzard; so quickly things change.

We search around in the storm for the top of Syme Ridge to begin our descent but are unable to find it, or discern any features in a world of white and grey. The storm increases in intensity and we're forced to take shelter on the eastern aspect, away from the now driving snow and stinging, wind-thrown graupel. Through a brief gap in the cloud we see, beneath us and off to the side, a glimpse of the ridge, and start an angling descent towards it, facing in and kicking our way down through the whiteness, but soon lose all orientation in the zero visibility.

After traversing for what feels like more than far enough towards the ridge, we make the call to descend directly to where we think it must be. Tiptoeing backwards, I come to a harder sheet of ice that starts to slope off. Feeling that there is a drop below us, I stop and secure myself to the ice, before lowering the rope into the gloom until its full length dangles sickeningly into nothing but air, the distance to the slope lost in a void of whiteness. We have ended up somewhere on the upper East Face, on the very edge of one of the gigantic ice cliffs that lurk there, and it comes to us that we're pushing too hard; that we should no longer be trying to descend, that we should be looking for shelter. We climb back up to the ridge, to the howling wind above.

We stand in the storm, there on the North Shoulder, looking into a crevasse. We need to get ourselves into it, away from the freezing wind that will, before long, take our lives, but it doesn't look very appealing. Finally, our choices dwindling, I jump into the deep snow at the bottom and there is an immediate respite. When I stomp along to the end of the crevasse, I see a long slope ramping further down into the mountain which, upon further investigation, opens into a small space. This, in a claustrophobic, ice-encased sort of way, will be where we spend the next three days.

For shelter we share a pack liner – a plastic bag, really – which is just big enough for the two of us to wriggle into. Every few hours one of us squeezes out, turns around and wriggles back in facing the other way. Lying on our packs and rope keeps us off the snow. We have about half a litre of water from which we take occasional swigs, topping it back up with ice chips each time and jamming it between us to prevent it from freezing. We have half a dozen barley sugars to share and are never warm, partly because Steve had dropped his pile jacket on the ascent, but mostly because it's just so cold. We have to get out of the bag often to fortify the wall of ice blocks we have been forced to build to keep the snow from above filling our little area. Only a vague half-light makes it down to us during the days, gloom interspersed with the darkness of the nights. We get to watch the rate of growth of each other's whiskers, up close, and also to know the bumps and angles of each other's shivering bodies. And, of course, contemplate what our fate might be.

On the third night it gets very cold. Out of optimism, we speculate that this is a good sign, that the weather must be swinging around to the south, the direction from which it will clear. In the morning we bust down our near ceiling height wall and the accumulated snow pours into our tiny room. It takes us half an hour to dig our way out up the snow cone behind it and when we reach the top, we discover that the crevasse has been filled in and that the weather has indeed cleared. We sit in the bright sunlight, in the deep new snow, and breathe again.

We're lucky: the snow, although thigh deep, has come with little wind. Even so, as we wade down Syme Ridge, huge powder snow avalanches erupt from the steeper faces on either side of us and

there is, among the grandeur, a feeling of smallness and trepidation
in our descent.

We collapse in the snow at the last unthreatened spot to contemplate
the final section. The traverse from the bottom of the ridge we are on to
the relative safety of the Plateau is known colloquially as 'the Mad Mile',
a broken and tortured section of glacier below the East Face of Tasman.
Covered thickly in new snow and avalanche debris from the storm cycle,
it's not going to be fast or easy or safe going, and we aren't in great
shape. We are, in particular, very thirsty and have been saving the few
remaining sips of water for the brief amount of relief they will provide
for the exertions of crossing the Mile. I reach for the water bottle.

And of all the events I remember from this trip, the one that occurs
next – and I don't remember who was responsible but I blame Steve – is
the one I remember the most clearly: the bottle, not placed in the snow
quite carefully enough, slides slowly down the slope and disappears into
the glacier below. It will be several hours of desperately thirsty work
until we make it back to the hut, but despite the urge to scream or cry
or go looking for the bottle, there's really nothing else to do except get
up and keep walking.

The thing that is hard

There is a point, in one's progression through mountaineering, that the
'thing'– the deep kernel of motivation or satisfaction or pleasure or
whatever it is that you get out of climbing, whatever keeps you returning
and looking for more – changes. It changes from the 'just being there'
of easier climbing, through the steepening of terrain and a heightened
sense of exposure and position, to where the climbing becomes
physically, mentally and genuinely hard; hard enough that you might fall
off and this falling would be a serious thing. It's at this point that a
change takes place and 'the thing' has to be put aside for a very real
here-and-now, in-your-face reality of consequence. It may occur to you

then, that there's a serious side to this amazing pastime you've discovered. You may question why you're pursuing this thing – for the sheer hell of it and not much more – when you don't really have to be here at all. Then again, you're young, and very, very keen, and you may not.

In 1986 Brian and I decided, perhaps a little precociously, that we were up for some harder climbing. Nestled into the head of the Hooker Glacier under the imposing Sheila Face of Aoraki/Mount Cook and the South Face of Hicks, is Empress Hut which, in the 1980s, was the base for climbing some of the biggest and hardest alpine routes in the country. Going big was what we had in mind; it seemed the obvious choice. Hicks in particular sports a range of steep and technical lines. About 500 metres high, the face is dark and steep, riven with thin runnels of ice even in summer. It seldom sees the sun and we plugged across the glacier through deep powder snow, cooled by the mountains' winter-shadow for a couple of hours before our arrival at Empress. Eyeing up the routes from the hut, across the bowl of the glacier, we were both intimidated and attracted.

'Line' could be described as an assessment of a route – its difficulty, its use of features, an intangible take on its merits. Like the fall-line of a skier, the drift of a fly fisher, it's an esoteric valuation that only other climbers can undertake. To someone looking at an existing route, line is all these things, and the lure of repeating a famously difficult route is a red rag to the young and the keen bull.

The route that most caught our eye the most was the Yankee-Kiwi Couloir, to which the guidebook gave its hardest grade of 6+. We didn't really know what that meant, but for those indefinable reasons of line, we were drawn towards this thin ice gully snaking up a great black wall of rock. The route would mostly be on ice. To climb the line we would have to link together a series of slim ribbons of white streaking the deeper contours of the face, but the continuity of the ice was broken in places where it had not been able to form, usually where it was too steep. Higher up the wall the ice looked more consistent, but there was a steep band on the second pitch where the lines of white broke up into small dots and the streaks around them turned clear and thread-like, barely covering the rock. It looked as though the rock overhung a little. It looked a little frightening.

As I stare up the second pitch, after a long and steep initial pitch, it starts to dawn on me what a hard lead actually means. It means that you don't really know how it's going to go up there. You can mentally piece together the way you'd like to go, or not, see where there might be some protection, or not, but you just can't know. The only way to find out is to start climbing until you arrive at the point, invariably, where you need – and here it becomes more than just a word – to commit. To continue, knowing that you can't climb down again; that you will make it up, or you will fall. This is where the fear starts. Fear is a thing that has its roots in the future – the 'what if' world of the mind. But that world contains other possibilities and whatever they may be, they are the reason I am here. Here at the beginning of the hard section, though, looking up the wall above, it's only the fear that is obvious.

The ice above Brian's belay is solid, which is a good start, but it runs out at the top of the gully we're in, which is capped by the steep wall. The black rock here is argillite which, as well as appearing unfriendly, is a slick and unreliable medium for climbing. Higher up to the left, ice dribbles down over the wall, indicating where the flow continues above, and although it looks shallow and patchy I'm drawn towards it. I climb until my feet are balancing on their front points in the last thin patch of gully ice and my hands are clinging to the untrustworthy rock, which now steepens and starts to lean me out past my point of balance. This is where it changes, right here. From here on, it will be hard.

I procrastinate by taking off my outer gloves for better dexterity and fiddle in some rock gear to protect the next moves – microwires wedged in an intermittent crack. Although small, they seem solid as I tug on them, clipping the rope, but the thing about gear like this is that you don't really know whether it will hold or not if you fall off. I look up, trying to shift my mind away from the nervousness toward something more positive, until there's nothing else to do but to move; to commit or to go down. Looking up, to the steepness and unknowingness of the wall above me, I begin.

I start by pulling on sharp-edged holds and stepping up, cramponed feet scraping insecurely on the rock, small scratches appearing on the surface of the slate-like stone. The noise of it seems harsh to me, wrong. Some internal guide tells me that the sound should be more firm and gritty, a compression, under my front points. I realise I need to place my feet more precisely onto the small edges in the rock and into the tiny slivers of ice they hold. With this focus my weight shifts more onto my feet and I feel myself come into a greater balance. As I move, the feeling comes to me at last that perhaps I could be equal to the climbing above me and that this is where I want to be, fear and all.

I make it to the first small drips of ice and reach for my ice tools, but discover that the melted-out and refrozen ice above has formed with water-drop indents and icicles, delicate features that initially suit my hands better than the picks; liquid turned to stone. The ice appears in discontinuous smears and intermittent blobs from which hang icicles, opaque formations with a light coating of tiny frost crystals that float off like dust motes as my hand grips each one, liner gloves sticking slightly to the frozen surface. Each blob is its own entity, separate and spaced well apart; the game will be to somehow join the dots. The climbing becomes strenuous, contortionist and completely absorbing.

There's an improbability in ice climbing that stems as much from the unlikeliness of trying to climb on frozen water, on an uncertainty of permanence, as from the situations you find yourself in. There's a physicality to steep ice, too – the swinging of axes and kicking of boots, the ice falling away as you strike it, the effort. In between those sections of awkwardness, though, in the constant struggle for balance, you need to move with precision and delicacy, to hook the pick just so, to trust a placement so much but no more, and nearly always with protection of unknown worth.

An ocean of detail appears before me: a small row of water droplet holes in a line – divots for my fingers, a small flake to stem my foot off, a notch between icicles to hook my pick into. The icicles to my side seem to collect the light and refract it towards me, but I focus on the detail I can use in front of me. I'm aware that the clearer icicles are more brittle, the opaque tops of the blobs more plastic, more accepting of my tools. In the deeper and thicker flows of ice there is colour, subtle variations of green and blue, or clear or white.

The look of the ice gives me a measure of how much I can trust it, how I can use it, how well it has adhered to the rock. The sound of the ice, too, when kicked or knocked, becomes a factor in the next move. Solid foot placements squeak underfoot as weight is shifted onto them, poorer ones have more of a soft crunchiness as they crumble. Best of all is a reassuring thunk as I kick my crampons into solid ice. The scratching, the tinkle of ice shards falling away below, the internal animal noises of exertion are the sounds I move by.

I find myself at the end of the blobby section, where the ice again becomes more of a thick sheen over the rock, more uniformly reliable – no less steep but somehow more understandable – and I begin to move more easily. I'm now high on the pitch. The mental world of assessment and decision has somehow, seamlessly, become movement, and I pause, comfortable now to look back down the pitch; down past the icicles I have slung as runners and the tiny finger pockets in the ice I used for holds, and the hardly perceptible scratch marks from my picks and front points. Down to Brian hanging on the belay, who is probably relieved that the pitch is doable after all, though he'll still be nervous. I also see wider than that, the whole of the pitch as a separate entity in itself, and past that to the drop of the face below us and the sweep of it above, out to the wider world, which is big and brawling and wild and mountainous and we're the only living things in it and right here and now, finely balanced on my toes, held in place by just a few centimetres of thin steel, with the rope falling away below me, it feels good to be in thrall to the moment in which you've cast off the suction of your world and the fears you hold within it, when you're here for the pure hell of it and nothing much more.

Worth it

The majority of trips to Aoraki/Mount Cook end in abject failure after lots of hard work, because of either dangerous conditions or fickle weather changes. But for several years I keep going back. In the face of the risks, hardships and failures, what makes something worth it?

There is a feeling of imminence in contemplating a big alpine route, and if it's a new route, there's also a sense of the unknown, an added frisson of excitement. Brian and I stand below the South Face of Aoraki, looking up and feeling small. Rising abruptly from the flatness of the upper Noeline Glacier, massive seracs hang over the centre of the face, obviously threatening. The steep wall to the right is an intimidating prospect too. Although we're not directly threatened by the ice cliffs, their looming presence adds to the atmosphere. The rock is dark, the aspect shady.

We are experiencing the strange conflict of emotions that precedes endeavours like this. It's not too late to change our minds, but the only reason would be fear; conditions look pretty good and the weather is fine. Thin intermittent lines of ice trickling down the wall suggest, rather than state, where to climb. The climbing looks difficult and there are many questions in our minds. It feels different, up here on the upper glacier. The air is cold and still, and has an extra clarity. There's some intangible feeling of removal, of specialness, to be considering what we intend to do. Much of this comes, perhaps, from the mana of the peak itself, the highest and proudest in the land.

The day is unforgettable. Patches and slivers of perfect snow ice fill the recesses of black rock. The climbing is delicate and absorbing, the route finding a constant puzzle. Far below us we see the buildings of Mount Cook village, and out beyond that the brown plains of Te Manahuna/the Mackenzie Country. It turns out that we're up to the challenge of the route, and we're pleased with our efforts. We called it something frivolous, but the feeling lodges in my heart: an early venture into the strange mix of ego, discovery and absorption in a place that is climbing a new route on a big mountain.

It's not just the hard routes that stay in the mind. The easiest route on Aoraki is also one of the most dangerous. The Linda Glacier falls from the summit in an enclosed trench, threatened at numerous points by unstable ice cliffs. The glacier is often broken by many crevasses and progress can be slow, which exposes you to more time under the seracs. I had sworn never to climb the mountain via this route, but there are times when conditions align to make the ascent a more reasonable proposition.

Jeremy and I find ourselves in Plateau Hut with a fine weather forecast, but facing the prospect of having to walk out because we have no more food. One of the guides in the hut recalls, jokingly, having buried a box of sausages in the snow at Empress Hut – on the other side of the mountain – and says we'd be welcome to it. The die is cast. We leave early in the morning to climb Aoraki, and in perfect conditions under a bright full moon, quickly dispatch the glacier. From a vantage point just below the summit, we watch the moon set over the ocean, just as the sun rises from the eastern flatlands. Topping out soon after, we complete the Grand Traverse and are back down at Empress Hut by 10 in the morning. The sausages are in the pan soon after. The day is a wonder of moving fast and light, of feeling fit and confident, of being in touch and easy with something big and grand. And ever since, I've had a taste for sausages.

❖

Winter trips are a big step up in difficulty and commitment, but there are rewards to be had. On Queen's Birthday Weekend in an early and cold winter, Steve, Dave, Al and I drive up from Dunedin in the morning, fly into the Plateau at lunchtime and climb the Zurbriggen Ridge on Aoraki in the cold shade of afternoon; the first winter ascent, as it turns out. The four of us dig a snow cave into the Linda Shelf and even without sleeping bags, manage to stay almost warm enough through the night. The next morning, having gone from sea level to over 3000 metres the previous afternoon, we're stricken with altitude sickness and feeling extremely tired; a rookie mistake. The upper mountain is in difficult condition, slick and tenuous, covered with hard ice but since the weather is perfect, we carry on.

In our debilitated state it takes us most of the day to climb to the top and along the summit ridge, all the way on bullet-hard, wind-carved ice. We choose to each move separately along the summit ridge towards the Middle Peak and I find myself falling behind the others as the daylight fades to night. My crampons and axes barely scratch the hard ice and I feel alone, small and desperately tired. Below me the country and the ocean all around it have already entered the cold dark of a winter's night. Above me the first stars are out, bright and seemingly very close. The knife edge of ice I'm on, the highest land for thousands of kilometres in any direction, catches the last long glance of the setting sun and becomes a glowing, jagged streak of blood-crimson, hanging for a few moments between the dark blue of the world below and the world above. And I am there, floating on it.

One of the other things that makes the mountains worth it, are your friends. Having finally caught up with the others at the Middle Peak 'schrund and prepared for a much colder, still sleeping bag-less bivvy (we had thought to be down off the mountain by this stage), I'm forced to announce that I've made a major mistake in the provisioning department and all the food we have left is half a block of almond-flavoured icing and a tin of sardines. I'll always remember the moment of collective comprehension that we were about to embark on a long period of enforced cold and hunger; how no one said a cross word and how we snuggled up close and brewed hot sweet icing drinks all night to ward off the deep freeze. The next day we completed the Grand Traverse to Low Peak, descended and shared our still frozen tin of sardines – one each – once we'd made it down to the glacier.

❖

Climbing on Aoraki means that you're higher than anything else on an already upthrust land. The North Ridge is a particularly exceptional position – a prow of weathered stone facing over the Tasman Sea, finishing directly at the summit. It's usually coated in a thick rime, the frozen breath of the sea-born westerlies, and the sense of exposure to the most extreme elements is clear.

Nick and I climb this, the route of the original ascent, in wintry conditions, on a cold and clear day. It's a long and absorbing route, never particularly easy, and we marvel at the first ascensionists of a century ago, who not only climbed up the route, but also back down it again, in hobnailed boots and with a hemp rope. I remember reaching the summit ice cap, and before climbing on towards the top and continuing along the Grand Traverse, looking back down the route. I imagine returning down it as that first party did; the sheer nerve of climbing back onto that rude height and, despite their hearts being in their mouths, the sense of mastery they must have felt.

This is another thing that climbing this mountain does: it hardens you up. To some degree this is an essential trait for an alpinist, and nothing achieves it better than the long down climb that is the standard descent on the western side of Aoraki. From the summit ridge to the flatness of the Empress Shelf, via Porters Col and the North West Couloir – all 1000 metres or so of vertical descent – never feels like a stroll. If conditions are reasonable, it's a technically simple down climb: just face into the slope and methodically stab your picks in, kick in with your front points, stab again, kick, repeat until, a few hours later, you reach the flatness of the glacier.

But it's always much more than that. It's usually afternoon when you get there. You've been on the move since before dawn and it's been hard work the whole way. It's too time consuming to use a rope, so you generally don't. The exposure yawns beneath your feet; it's too steep for self-arresting and there can be no trips or slips. The descent goes on and on, a constant trade-off between how firmly you place your tools and how much energy you use up, the size of your steps and how fast you try to move; security versus efficiency. The afternoon sun alters the snow from hard to soft as you descend; the type of insecurity changes. You change your grip on the axes to accommodate the changes in snow texture, rest with your feet sideways at regular intervals, wipe the sweat from your eyes and get used to the points of your crampons and axes losing their grip occasionally, sliding before they grab in the softening snow.

As you near the bottom, the risk of rockfall increases as the snow loosens its hold on the rocks embedded in it. There are lower angle sections here and you feel you want to turn around and crab sideways or face outwards even – anything to make it go faster. But you're tired now and you have to be careful: the efforts of the day have worn you down; it's harder to concentrate. You get to the 'schrund at the bottom of the descent gully and just want to jump it, to land in the soft snow on the far side and make it to the safety of the glacier, to be done with it. You know you should abseil but that means cutting a bollard and all you really want is for it to end, to be safe, but once again you've got to do the right thing to ensure you don't fuck it up. You're an alpinist now.

Despite the eventual successes, though, the near misses add up. Like the time a serac fall from high on the South Face wiped out our approach tracks at the bottom of White Dream, barely a few minutes after we had made them. Or the rockfall off the South Ridge that had us running for our lives across the upper Noeline Glacier, as rocks overtook us and dust stained the snow dark behind us. Another time, when approaching the bottom of the West Face of Dixon in the half-light of morning and a thick mist, we heard a muffled boom from far above us, somewhere high on Tasman. We stopped and listened and, hearing no more, continued across the flat glacier. A fridge-sized chunk of ice then appeared out of the gloom, bounced quickly between us and disappeared again, almost without a sound. Well, that was funny... Another time, high in the Yankee-Kiwi Couloir, I bridged carefully past the sharp-edged flake of rock that sat precariously on its tiny ledge, not touching it at all, but it fell off anyway after I'd passed, scything past Brian and nearly killing him at his belay. Or abseiling the descent route on Hicks late one afternoon when a large sheet of rime broke off high above me, smashing into a thousand pieces immediately in front of my stance. And all the other times that nothing fell down, but could have.

For a while, these things became something other – incidentals, gripping yarns at dinner parties – but increasingly I started to question what was really worth it. I moved to Wānaka, started a family, a business and discovered the attractions of the Aspiring region. I visited Aoraki less often, whittling down the routes I still wanted to do before leaving for good, until there was only one.

The McInnes Ridge of Nazomi rises proudly from the lower Hooker Glacier all the way to the summit. From there a short ridgeline drops down to the col that joins it to the South Ridge of Aoraki, which rises directly to Low Peak and the beginning of the Grand Traverse. It would be a link-up of the bigger features I hadn't climbed yet, and ending at the summit of Aoraki. I need to be up there one more time, just one more time along that highest mile; just one more Grand Traverse.

Laetitia and I are high on the McInnes, soloing the mixed ground below the ridgeline. I'm 20 metres or so above her, out of sight, when I hear a high-pitched request for help – now. I scratch across on some hard ice and tricky terrain until I can see her predicament. Her shoulder has dislocated during some awkward manoeuvre and she's stuck in a tenuous situation, unable to move. I organise a quick anchor and lower the rope to her. Once secured to the rope she's able to relocate her errant shoulder and, in usual Laetitia style, is keen to continue. I'm keen too but cast my mind to the route ahead, to the long slopes we will be soloing, the 2000 metres of elevation we have yet to gain; continuing isn't a sensible option. Giving it away isn't easy, though. Conditions and weather are fabulous, but I only have to think 'What if?' – what if this happened again on the summit ridge, or just about anywhere up high – to shake my head and make the call to descend. Reluctantly. Again.

We spend the night bivvied out and retreat the next day via a convoluted and dangerous route through the lower Noeline Icefall. Above us, the South Ridge of Aoraki is in obviously terrific condition and I have to shake the urge away; it can happen again, just wait for it to be right.

The next attempt is with Rich, a year or two later. The weather forecast is good, the conditions less so, but I can't wait. Still, after all these years, that inexplicable, stomach-deep urge for a particular feature.

We climb fast and well, but top out on Nazomi into obviously deteriorating weather. The sky to the west is dark with moisture. A massive lenticular is draped over the summit ridge of Aoraki and the wind strains hard at us, hard enough to be blowing small stones from off the ridge. There is no question of continuing and it doesn't matter anyway. Finally I've had enough of everything climbing here is – hard, dangerous work with a high failure rate. There will be no fairy tale ending. We begin the descent into what will soon be rain, knowing it will be an unpleasant day. There will be loose rock, a broken-up glacier and a walk out in shitty conditions, as there always is here. I am leaving.

I stop and wait for Richard, bending forward and resting my elbows on my thighs, the classic pose for briefly taking the weight of your pack off your shoulders. Buried among the moraine rocks at my feet is an old-style mountaineering boot but I'm too tired to reach down and investigate, my mind still in the half-trance state of a numbing walk out.

Richard arrives and also adopts the position. The water drips from our hoods onto the ice and I look again at the old boot.

'Bet that could tell a few stories,' I say.

Richard reaches down, works the boot from out of the rocks and peers inside. 'Yep,' he says and passes it to me so I, too, can register that inside is a foot. Old and kind of messy, mixed in with gravel, but without doubt a foot.

We raise our eyes and look around. The world is grey and wet. Pools of meltwater sit on the dirty ice between mounds of gritty broken rock. It is a somewhat forlorn scene, made more so as we notice more artefacts of a life lying on the ice, or protruding from sodden patches of old snow.

We put our packs down and wander around, registering a range of items: a piton and carabiner attached to an old etrier, an ice screw like an old bottle opener and a heavy knitted jumper, the sort you make for your grandson to keep him warm in the mountains. There are bones too, lots of small bones. I find a larger one freshly melted out from a snow patch, smooth and white, and then another. I realise they are almost identical – both right femurs. That makes it two people, then, whose legs used to be strong and muscular and attached to their bodies like ours. We can't help but speculate about who they might be.

We make a small pile of what we have found and a cairn of rocks to mark it, not really knowing what else to do. We look around and make a note, as best we can in the monochrome similarity of the lower glacier, of where the remains lie. I suppose we'll tell somebody. The rain remains steady as we shoulder our packs and continue down the valley, some favour of the universe allowing us, rather than them, to return home.

PART THREE

SCHIST

Schist is a step up from greywacke. For starters it's beautiful, shot through with depths of colour and microcosmic flecks of mica, spatters and veins of quartz. It weathers to beautiful shapes, lashed by the harsh elements of Otago and Westland: the waters of rain, ice and river, and the wind of high places. It's often different in its final form – a character rock.

Formed from the same sources as greywacke, the depositions of the land before, schist has been pushed back down and reimagined in the deeper crucibles of the earth. Pressured and twisted, it has then cooled, resurfacing in the Southern Alps/Kā Tiritiri o te Moana to be carved into the landscapes we play among, think about at night and occasionally die in surrounded by its beauty.

Schist's reliability provides fabulous venues for climbing and the beautiful shapes it forms – from huge exposed mountain walls to the smallest finger pockets – keep me intrigued for a long while.

The mountains are schist, the crags that line the side walls of the valleys are schist, the canyons I explore and become my workplace are schist. The way it often weathers into flat-sided rocks also makes it ideal for construction of all sorts. I have built my garden walls with stacks of it, and scoured local beaches for the plates that became the pathways for my house, the flagstones surrounding my hearth. For me, schist is the bedrock of home.

Home ground

We arrived in Wānaka, my partner Ros and I, in 1993, in an old car swaying with load, enough gear for a ski season and enough money to avoid working for a few months. We stayed, of course, for good. The people were different – mountain people instead of students, lifestylers rather than careerists – and everyone seemed involved with the landscape around them. We became like that too: making a living among mountain, ski and canyon guides, pursuing in our spare time the same activities as in our work time. There was always someone to get keen with and every day, driving the Mātukituki road, on the way to work or play 'up the valley', we would see this fabulous mountain.

Mount Aspiring/Tititea emerges from the landscape almost as a peak from a fantasy novel. Rising abruptly and elegantly from its glacial plateau, surrounded by an encircling ring of lesser peaks, it looks almost cartoonish from certain angles, in its symmetry and sharpness. To anybody, climber or not, it fits the popular idea of a beautiful mountain. For Māori, Tititea – the glistening mountain, an ancient ancestor – has for centuries been a prominent waypoint and marker, often edged with snow-shine and seen from many places, a link between the celestial world and the world of living people. So to anyone, climber or not, it means something, this mountain.

My first attempts at adventure were, of course, directly related to the peak itself, without warm-up or reserve. I was rebuffed, often, but I kept returning, until I felt at home. The routes on Aspiring are classic – so classic that when I finally did succeed I climbed the South-west Ridge several times. I failed to climb the South Face a lot, before returning there, and succeeding, more than once. Not until I got the classic routes out of the way did I see the obvious – that 90 per cent of climbers went to 10 per cent of the terrain and there was a lot left to explore. I resolved not to be one of them, and putting the obvious excitements behind me allowed me to start looking around. I liked what I saw.

An early trans-alpine traverse of the region around Aspiring opened my eyes to the breadth of options. Over an Easter when the snow stayed frozen and hard throughout, Brian and I started from the Kitchener Cirque and climbed a narrow and forested spur to Moncrieff Col. Crossing to the western side of the Main Divide felt like stepping into another land. We traversed the Volta Ice Field, aiming for the dramatic pyramid of Aspiring, and bivvied under the North-east Face, lying beneath bright constellations, soaking up the feel of wilderness. The next morning we made an attempt on the elegant spur above us, but found it too difficult without rock shoes. After retreating, we crossed the Main Divide for a second time via Popes Nose, abseiling down onto the expanse of the Bonar Glacier. We then dropped via the evocatively named Flightdeck onto the Maud Francis Glacier, and traversed around to the high col between Mount Avalanche and Rob Roy. Here we bivvied again, as the sun set and a full moon rose in perfect asymmetry, before threading a way next morning through the crevasses of the Avalanche Glacier to Rob Roy saddle.

I was so excited, on this first visit. I would return to each of these venues several times: the North-east Face of Aspiring, the East Face of Popes Nose, the South Face of Rob Roy.

Despite being visible from the lakefront in Wānaka, and close to the road end, Rob Roy is a much underrated peak, walked past and ignored by the masses intent on climbing Aspiring, further up the valley. It is, in fact, a proud and complex massif, and the vertical height gain means any ambitions to climb it require hard work. Surrounded by complex glaciers, the slabby northern aspects contrast sharply with the vertiginous wall of the South Face, demarcated by the blade of the kilometre-long summit ridge. Allan had told me about the summit ridge, in particular its razor sharpness and rock towers: 'It's a gripper.'

Sitting on the summit and looking along that ridge, I have to admit that it seemed an accurate description. It hasn't kept Allan away, though; he's sitting here next to me on the summit of Rob Roy, hooking into a large chilli-bean pizza from the local cafe – the joys of a peak close to home – and we had left the car not long after first light to get to here for our late lunch. So far there has been a long grind up a rocky gully, and some complicated route-finding through a glacier riddled with enormous, yawning crevasses. The next bit, involving the summit ridge, looks as though it will require a bit of finesse.

Adding to the amount of grippage we feel is that fact that, in our lightweight quest to traverse Rob Roy in a day, we don't have a rope. Allan had estimated that, despite its obvious sharpness, the ridge probably wouldn't need that type of security, and although things often seem different on closer inspection, there seems little to do but carry on regardless. We polish off the last of the pizza and get on with it.

Allan is right on both counts: the ridge is indeed a gripper and it is doable without a rope. In fact, a rope would be quite a hindrance on the convoluted terrain we're traversing. The situation is tremendous, the sense of exposure amplified by the enormous drops on either side and the seemingly precarious nature of the ridge's make-up. The ridge itself is a serrated blade; between the high points are wedged large blocks. At one stage, climbing along on a thin slice of rock, hands gripping the top edge and looking for footholds, I realise that I can see right through the ridge below me; the stone I'm clinging to is simply one of those blocks. Feeling as though you are hanging onto something that seems to be unattached to anything else certainly adds to the sense of exposure.

For all that, though, the rock is solid and trustworthy and we make good time. It's an early hint that spectacular terrain doesn't necessarily require a whole lot of equipment; that it's often better without. The rest of the traverse continues smoothly, the terrain manageable,

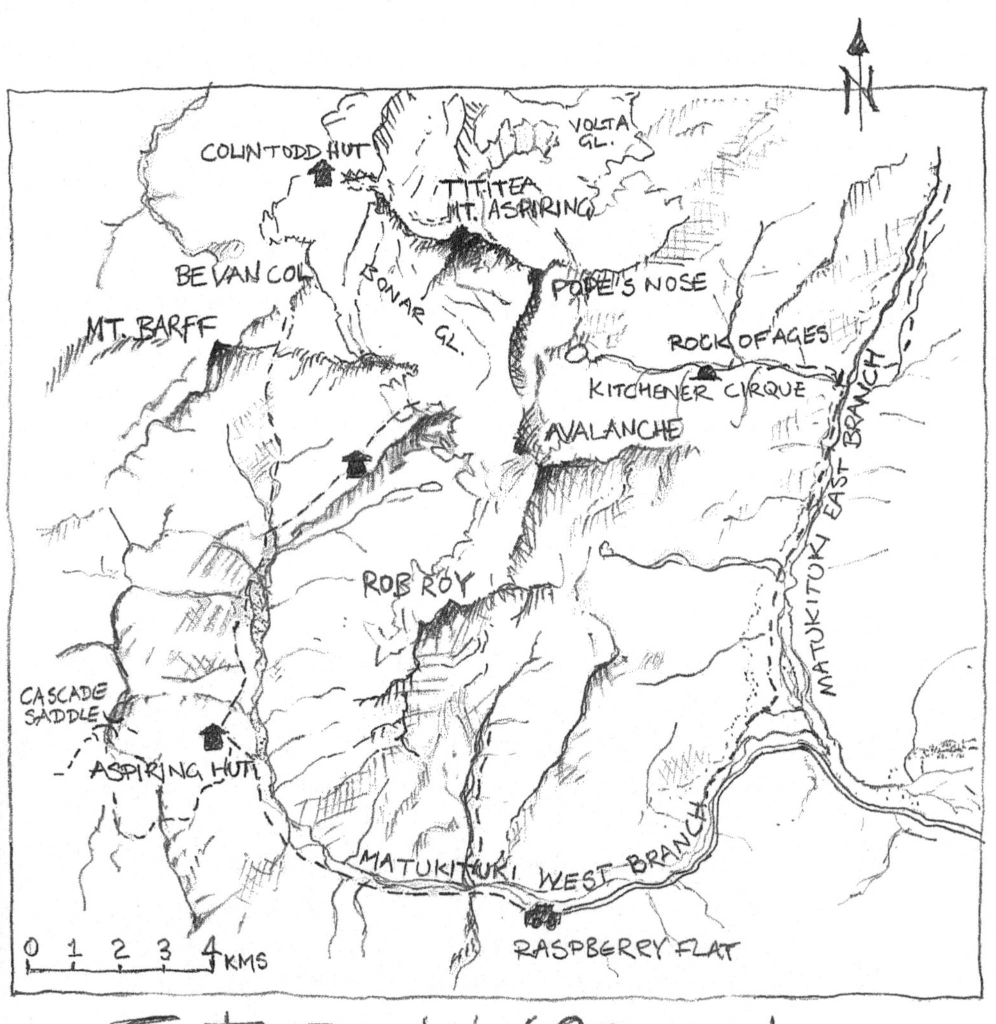

TITITEA/ASPIRING

the situation fine. As we descend from the Low Peak, I'm ahead when I arrive at a tricky-looking section. I spend time climbing back and forth, working out a route. Finally down safely on a soft snow patch, I'm about to yell up to Allan that it may well be easier to just jump, when he lands heavily in the slush next to me, having worked it out for himself. Moving fast is infectious, and fun.

We're back at the car in good time, feeling well chuffed with ourselves. We've done something no one else has and we're full of ideas for future missions. Descending the valley, all we've been able to talk about was the South Face looming above us.

The next time we arrive at the summit ridge it's midwinter, everything coated in a frozen whiteness. The afternoon is moving on and the temperature is plummeting. We're tired and there's a long way still to go. The traverse of the summit ridge, which we had thought would be a magnificent gesture of flamboyance on which to finish the South Face, looks sharper and more uncompromising than ever. There is no pizza. Behind us lie two big days, two cold bivvies and 20-odd pitches of steep ice climbing on the face. Before us lies another rough bivvy followed by a long descent around the mountain – and the summit ridge.

It seems something of an extravagance to continue along the ridge after what we've just done, but it does look spectacular, coated in weird rime formations that make it seem otherworldly, more like some Andean monster than something so close to home. We have some time in hand, so decide to give it a go anyway; at least we have a rope this time.

It takes no more than a rope length for us to decide that the ridge isn't something we can climb. Progress will be tenuous, and slow, and we'll be here until well after dark if we continue, if we haven't fallen off before that. Rather than reverse the section we've just climbed, we decide to abseil down the northern side, into the arriving night. We make it to the glacier as darkness falls and have time to make a quick brew before the wind picks up, driving us into our separate cocoons to weather the incoming storm. Before long, the night becomes hellish. The wind picks up, screaming around us and blasting us with graupel. We're slowly drifted into the moving snow until we lie half-buried, shivering and unmoving, with nowhere else to go until daylight.

The morning brings a rapid change of fortune. After a brutal struggle to get organised within the confines of our bivvy bags, we simultaneously stand up to discover that we're not in the grip of a major storm but, rather, have been lying in a ground blizzard that comes up to not far above our knees. Allan and I look at each other and laugh out loud.

Conditions are still difficult but our retreat isn't the epic we had expected. Buffeted by the nor-wester, we retrace the steps of my recce trip of several years ago, across the Avalanche Glacier and down the Rob Roy Valley, a retreat from winter and a return to spring. We return to Wānaka, only a short drive down the valley to our friends and families. We travel through forests, alongside rivers and canyons, and everything along the way is a bright reminder of home.

❖

Somewhere along the line, my university studies had fallen by the wayside, replaced with a hard-earned qualification in mountaineering, and soon after we moved to Wānaka these skills became usefully translated into a business venture. The last ice age had left behind it physical features of steep-sided valleys, incised by deep gorges cut by the surging meltwaters of the retreating glaciers. After a climbing trip to France introduced us to canyoning, Ros and I decided to start a business in Wānaka where, as it turned out, the canyons were spectacular, every bit as good as their fabled European counterparts. The exploration of these schist gorges, deep, steep and technical, added a real excitement to our endeavours, proved an ideal testing ground for my skills and strengthened our relationship with the local landscape.

The mid-1990s were a golden time to start an adventure based business. We were able to make it up as we went, with a refreshing lack of government oversight. Deep Canyon began as a good idea, an attempt to combine the fun of canyoning with the need to earn money, but it soon became something bigger, an integral part of our lives. It became apparent that many of our customers were having more than a good time; that their hands-on interactions with nature were often profoundly moving experiences. Like us when we explored new canyons or discovered new climbs, they felt in touch with something special. The joy of making it up as we went along became tempered by the inevitable encroachment of bureaucracy, and the constant balancing of the realities of running a business sometimes made work seem like a chore. But the people themselves, and the feeling that we were doing something worthwhile, kept us going, and we gradually reached an acceptable level of ease in the running of our business life.

Personal life became more complicated too. Monty was born just as we were starting the business which, although it seemed a natural and beautiful progression to life, also seemed to add a weight of responsibility, and the initial wonders of a happy childhood period became slowly more complex. Ros and I struggled through it, each in our own way. My method of coping, when it all got too much, was to head for the mountains on my doorstep. I went there often for renewal and refreshment, and for a long while this was all I needed. But at some point, a much harsher reality intruded on the simplicity of mountain life and heading off no longer seemed so simple. The local peaks brought me life but they also introduced me, rudely and abruptly, to death.

The thing that is really hard

There is one thing that most long-time alpinists share – the gaps in our lives where friends used to be. Death in the mountains is a given for some of those who spend time there, a kind of numbers game;

the statistical arena in which mountaineers live and die. Tragedy is an inherent part of wildness and I've had to learn to live with it. Gradually, I've reached some kind of ease with this aspect of life; an acceptance of consequences and a sense that a mountain life will be worth it for some, but not others. But at the time death stings hard, and through all these years I thought to myself – often – that maybe I'd had enough.

It had started as a mission of my own, of planning to solo the Coxcomb Ridge on Aspiring. I had the urge, the great idea that would scratch the itch, for now at least. It was all planned for Labour Weekend – conditions and weather looked good – but on the very eve of leaving I bumped into Hugh. Now I love my friends, so when Hugh suggested that I be more sociable and that as he, Rob and Danny were thinking of going climbing anyway, I should hook up with them for the Coxcomb. So, in the way things do, the mission morphed from the intensity of my personal ideal to the easier and more social one of a 'foursey' on the Coxcomb. It wasn't what I'd wanted, not deep down, but it would be fun. Perhaps this was the first mistake.

Alpine starts have never agreed with me – muesli at 2 a.m. I find unbearable – but the feeling of grossness usually wears off by the time it gets light. This morning is different, however. Even as we cross the magnificence of the upper Bonar Glacier into the light of a beautiful day, my stomach clenches in spasm. I throw up my breakfast onto the hard frozen snow of the glacier, again into the crevasse at the bottom of the approach slope and again when we reach the crest of the ridge itself.

Feeling after a short rest that I might have finished with sickness, we continue along the ridge and start the climbing proper, managing a couple of pitches before I spew some more and then fall asleep for half an hour on a ledge now being touched by the early sun. The boys let me rest and, being in a social and relaxed mode, they decide not to continue either. It's reassuring to have them there.

The decision, an easy one, is made to descend and an abseil or two brings us back to the flatness of the glacier. An idea is mooted – and it's pretty much wholly mine but everyone agrees to it – to wander over to the top of the headwall of the Kitchener Cirque and try to get a look down a route I'd been looking at: the East Face of Popes Nose. Then, I muse, we can head along the top edge of the glacier, end up over at the bottom of the West Face of Avalanche and if I feel better by then, maybe we could climb that instead. It seems a reasonable plan, with potential for some interest and a way to claw back some reward for our efforts.

We walk over to the edge of the Bonar, to where the upper edge of the glacier cleaves suddenly off into nothingness, a keen and ragged demarcation from the flatness of the glacier to the massive verticality below it. It's hard to find a decent viewpoint to look into the Kitchener. Huge cornices have formed along the edge of the glacier, the warmth of the summer sun yet to arrive and trigger their demise. Required to take care, we end up perched on a rocky outcrop, peering over the edge. We aren't really able to see much of the face but we can feel the draw of the void below. I start to experience again some germ of the drive I'd had before getting sick. Feeling the need to shake off the physical and mental frustrations of the morning, I leave the others on the outcrop admiring the view and walk on ahead, forging a track by myself across the glacier, in the now softening snow.

An hour or so later, I'm sitting by myself at the far end of the wall below Mount Avalanche. The sun warms me and a faint breeze floats up the glacier, bringing an air of peace and beauty to the day, but it's not a feeling I can enjoy. I look back at my tracks, an irregular dotted line threaded along the top edge of the Bonar. They seem almost reckless in their proximity to the top of the wall, even though I'd been careful. The sick feeling that had been hanging in my guts earlier has gone, replaced, slowly, by another, even worse one.

Following in my footsteps are two figures and I assume, for as long as I can, that the missing person is just hidden behind a roll of the glacier or has gone a different way, even though this is impossible without my seeing them. I wait as the others come closer, willing the third person to just appear, and it isn't until the others draw near that I know who isn't there, who had broken through one of those giant cornices to fall into that huge empty space, from a perfectly flat piece of glacier. It had been my idea to go to the edge of the Bonar. I'd put in the tracks. Did the cornice break from my steps or theirs?

It is Danny who doesn't arrive with the others, Danny who has disappeared from our lives, Danny that we will never see again. The horror is written on the faces of Hugh and Rob before they reach me – the shock, the waste, the uselessness. Years later I still think about it, whether to feel stupid, or sorry, or just sad; to take some part of the blame, or put it down to dumb bad luck, or some combination of both. But even after all this time, I don't know what to make of it; whether there's a mistake there to learn from, or not. I am still here, the mountain is still here, Danny is not.

May isn't a conventional month in which to go mountaineering. The crevasses remain unfilled by the winter snow yet to arrive, although enough has usually fallen to make conditions unpleasant. The days are short, the weather is cold and often unsettled; it's a good time to get caught out in the first big storm of winter. May is also the month of the inversion in Wānaka, when a heavy layer of fog blankets the lake basin and people move around under a grey and oppressive cloud. If you can get above the fog, however, the view is of ranges of jagged peaks rising from a cotton-wool ocean, all bathed in the bright light of the winter sun. Higher than all the others is Tititea, or as I knew it then, Aspiring, and on those days when the mountain isn't hidden by fog, the South Face – the shady ice-covered one – is the aspect you see.

I hadn't met Gordy much – usually between the speakers on the dance floor when the music was hardest and we both happened to open our eyes at the same moment – but he didn't seem the sort of guy to be a receptacle of conventional wisdom. He carried an air of unconcerned wildness, and it turned out that he was often keen for a mission when no one else was. There were times when some seething desire for action meant I had to get out there too, so we had that in common. I had no idea if he was much of a climber, but sometimes just having someone to share the energy is all you need, and if that someone hits the dance floor as hard as you do, then that has to be a good place to start.

It took two days to get to Colin Todd Hut in May. The valley was quiet under a frosted shade and there was a feeling of purity. The Mātukituki was empty of people. We saw no one on the way in and there was no one at the hut. Best of all, the weather was perfect and conditions were excellent. We left the hut under the sharp glint of winter stars and the snow was crisp and hard. Staying hard up against the flank of the mountain we traced a tight line through the crevasses of the Bonar, crossed the South-west Ridge as the light came to the day, down climbed a convenient ramp on the other side and found ourselves at the base of the South Face – a quick, effective and unconventional approach. I still had no real idea of how much climbing Gordy had actually done, but he seemed naturally competent and we were working well together. Things were panning out nicely.

Traversing along beneath the sheer bulk of the South Face would normally have felt intimidating, but on this day it felt as if we were meandering along on some kind of alpine boulevard. Some vagary of the conditions had arranged to create a footpath-like feature along the whole of the bottom of the face and we strolled along like country gentlemen on a relaxing jaunt. There were several beautiful ice lines falling over the steep lower band of the face, all obviously in fantastic shape, and we found it so hard to choose that we ended up at the far end of the face still undecided. I had the impression that I could have pointed at the most unlikely smear of overhanging desperateness and Gordy would have said yes. Or, more likely, 'Hell yeah!'

We pick an existing route known as the Chocolate Fish Route, because it looks the most fun. It's a narrow and defined line that runs straight up the right-hand side of the face to exit onto the Coxcomb Ridge, which also looks interesting in the winter conditions, razor-edged and rimed up. The ice is in that squeaky, 'flick and stick' condition that transforms ice climbing from serious to serious fun; the ice steep and perfect, the rock clean and dry. We swap leads the whole way up, climbing relaxed and fast and topping out onto the ridge with plenty of daylight to spare – always a good thing when there's still a way to go.

The top section of the Coxcomb is a marvellous place, nearly as high as the summit. The rock is solid and weathered and the ridge sports some interesting terrain, such as the World's Most Exciting 5-Metre Abseil. We arrive at this feature on a bit of a roll, which may explain Gordy's enthusiasm to 'just jump it'. I can see his point – a quick run in crampons down an icy slab and a leap across a gut-wrenching void onto a small pillow of snow stuck to a razorback ridge would definitely save some time – but wisdom prevails. Even so, the alternative abseil punches above its weight, since you have to swing furiously back and forth to get back onto the ridge – all the while dangling out over the South Face as the rope rubs on a vicious sharp overhang.

We were on the summit by late afternoon, which was good going in the short days of May. Gordy had been a great partner, fast, solid and good fun. We stopped and rested for a while, with the clouds building from the lowlands below us and the long descent ahead, and, for the first time, felt a bit tired. But I wasn't worried and neither was Gordy. The North-west Ridge shone golden and hard in the late afternoon light below us, weathered into a glistening sheet of clear ice, like a glass catwalk. The descent could easily have felt insecure but I'll always remember the confident ease with which Gordy strolled down that bright ridge – with golden towers of cloud rising around us and the world below us already in the evening's winter-shadow – as if he was born to do just that thing.

Gordy died in the mountains, only a short year or two after that May ascent of Aspiring. He died climbing by himself on Mount Tasman and

the only mistake he made was being just a little too keen, a concept that
I doubt had ever occurred to him. One thing I will never think, though,
is that Gordy's mistake was to become a mountaineer.

❖

It seems a long way from the valley floor to where I am now, a long
and arduous way. The soft light of the morning's full moon has been
replaced with the harshness of snow-reflected sunlight. There has been
a lot of physicality between now and then and I'm forced to stop. I feel
weak and trembly, overstretched. Something isn't right.

Above me the rime-encrusted ridge up to the West Peak of
Mount Earnslaw/Pikirakatahi looks unfavourable. Although it's Easter
and late in the summer season, a thick smattering of new snow covers
the dark rock. Conditions are less than ideal and when you're on your
own, it's best that they are. Enthusiasm wanes, even as it becomes a
full-blown beautiful day. Inwardly I sigh, but resolve to head down while
conditions are good; the sun is starting to soften the large snowfield on
which I'm standing.

As I descend over a small roll-over, the snow becomes firmer again
and with no crampons on, I started plunging my heels in harder,
working to maintain grip. I know instantly what the sudden pistol shot
behind me means, and feel the quick release of tension in the slope
underfoot. Turning quickly, I try to plunge my axe in above the fracture
line, but the crack is metres above me. There is a moment of dawning
comprehension, just long enough to start taking in the enormity of
what's happening, before the snowfield begins to break up all around
me, seemingly in slow motion, hard slabs of snow buckling and heaving
like a cartoon earthquake.

Time morphs into a different speed, almost slow-motion. There
seems to be no sound. I start to lose my feet in the now shifting snow
and find myself twisted around, facing down the slope. Below me the

valley floor is very distant. The stories of your life playing before your eyes and the instant sadnesses are all true. I see my death right there as if it has already happened: my family, my friends, the funeral even, an alternative reality waiting to be taken. A scream forces itself from somewhere deep inside me as I struggle, the now sliding snow dragging on my legs, pulling me into it.

I throw myself forward in a frenzied physical effort that lands me on my stomach, and find myself sliding fast in front of the ever-growing chaos behind me, before somersaulting wildly and somehow ending up on my feet. Down and across, with the slope breaking up above me, I run, harder than I've ever run before. Eventually, legs whirling like that *Looney Tunes* Roadrunner, I outrun the avalanche to the side, over a shallow ridge. Many tonnes of snow sweep my tracks, some to pile up in a flat area at the top of the bluffs, most to carry on roaring and grinding, for a long time, down to the distant valley.

I spend the next few hours only a couple of hundred metres away from the snowfield, lying in an alpine pasture, savouring small things. That night I light a fire in the valley and have a little party all by myself. I find a piece of schist in the stream, the exact size and shape of a club; I have it still, as some kind of reminder.

As I'm driving home the next day, a car comes towards me at speed on the wrong side of the road, and I'm forced to swerve violently into the grass to avoid the collision. The other vehicle doesn't stop. I sit unscathed in the car, tilted over in the roadside ditch and for a while nothing happens until, from somewhere deep inside – the same place the scream came from in the avalanche – I start to laugh hysterically, and it takes some time before I'm able to stop.

Afterwards, I work out the technicalities of the avalanche. A cold fine spell had preceded the storm and the wind-loaded snow from this had been followed by several days of sun and cold nights. Melt and thaw of the new snow on top had formed a hard slab over the frosted layer beneath it – the weakness on which the snowpack had slid. Obvious in theory, but a very unusual occurrence in reality. Firm snow at the end of summer? The last slope before the tussock?

I doubt a single one of my avalanche expert friends would have had concerns about the stability of that slope. They might have died there as I so nearly did. They might not have seen that car coming at them either. You can never be too careful, and likewise, you can never really know.

The rain's coming, dark sheets moving down the lake. The first fat drops pop dust into the air, soon beaten down and swamped. Summer smells, rain at last. A long-standing westerly brings this rain. It started on the day they died, 'Hip' and Paul, and their client Dave. We are, many of us, grieving. For days long banners of storm cloud stretch from the mountains, wind shaped and lit by golden sunsets. Always beautiful, always reminding.

It's circus night in town, New Year's Eve 2003. Everything is a reminder; the circus acrobats are strong, confident and athletic, like him. The crowds of excited children – everyone with kids around here has a 'Hip' story. The mountains remind us too, and the wind-seethed lake. He seems everywhere. Perhaps he is.

We finished hacking out a spectacular razor blade of snow, turned into an atmospheric and comfortable bivvy spot. The day's climbing had gone well too, with no dramas and plenty of big grins. The crux had been Dave's. Unable to reach the holds above from a small ledge, he had slapped and teetered his way up a blunt arête to a flake; powerful and off-balance moves. I'd wondered if he was going to fall off. Seconding past the same spot and being taller, I just reached up, grabbed the flake and carried on. It drew some laughs.

After settling in, Dave pulled out the cell phone. It hadn't occurred to me to bring one but his experience of this part of the mountains meant he knew there would be a small window of reception. It was party night at home and when we called preparations were in progress; there was small talk with lovers. Our little crest seemed even more homely. We talked, relaxed, revelled in the closeness. The West Face of Tasman seemed a long way from the dance floor, far above the moonlit snowfields and ocean, close to the winter stars, to a great big universe.

Next morning the rope lengths above the bivvy were absorbing and sustained, crampons scratching on solid rock, knocking off thin chips of rime as we climbed. We savoured the height gained, the fall away below, glacier becoming ocean. The top of the buttress was a mini summit. We took photos; I became a poster pin-up for Dave's guiding company. We laughed some more.

The exit pitch climbed around a spectacular cleft in the ice of the North Shoulder, a dramatic finish to the route. The top was expansive, relaxing, a quiet buzz. The ridge was firm winter snow, ideal for the descent. We faced in, front pointing down and across, the climbing simple enough but the exposure a constant force. Conditions were stable, the wind breathless. Or maybe just holding its breath; we crossed the place where, three years later, a small avalanche would cut away, and Dave's life would be taken. But on that day – that perfect day – we felt masters of our destinies. The descent was a joy. There was no pressure, just concentration. No worry, only awareness; we soaked it all up. From the deck of the hut, we watched the sun sink into the sea, blood over water. It was beautiful. Thanks Hip.

Search and rescue work – dealing with the consequences of other people's accidents – adds another perspective to death in the mountains. Other people died climbing too, not just my friends, and I have developed a kind of ease with it. It is the price that someone, sometime, is going to pay, seemingly again and again.

It is late afternoon by the time we arrive at Aspiring, the view from the helicopter confirming the report we'd received: a climber fallen on the Ramp. There's no body apparent this time, just a broken gash in the 'schrund below the face. Although the outcome looks likely to be the same as the last time I was here, it's only been a short time since the accident was reported and there's an urgency to investigate, a chance of survival. A maybe.

We hover as I try to identify a spot handy to the site that is free from crevasses, eventually settling on an area of smooth snow that looks safe. We land, unload and the machine lifts off, leaving us to the quiet of the mountain – a practical consideration but also one that seems to reflect the gravity of the situation.

My foot immediately breaks through into a hidden crack and we have to spend time safeguarding ourselves where we are; never make the situation worse. As quickly as we can, we fix anchors so I can be belayed over to the lip of the 'schrund. Before entering it I look around. The sun still has some warmth in it but the snow underfoot is firm – ideal conditions for climbing. There would have been a sense of excitement setting off in the morning.

I leave the sunlight and abseil into the shade of the crevasse, into a cold underworld. There's a sense of anticipation, the hope that there will be a reply to my shouted questions. But there's no answer, just an absence. He's not far down. The body is twisted and crumpled, jammed hard into a confined space where the walls of the crevasse come together. Snow has fallen down with the body and partially covered it; blood has soaked into the whiteness. I climb back out of the crevasse before lowering in the officials – the medic and police. Death must be certified.

This all takes time and as I sit out on the glacier minding the ropes, the sun moves into the later stages of the day, slowly softening the light to a mellow golden hue. Below the icefall, beyond the living ranges, the ocean burns in the west, and the electric blue shadows of the crevasses around us seem of a different world. It is very peaceful; the only sounds are the ones we generate ourselves. Little is said.

The body is recovered and put into the bag designed for just this task. It is an awkward package and handling isn't as respectful as we would like. We all feel the depth of the situation and mark it our own ways; quiet words are addressed, whether spoken or not. The machine comes back in to pick us up. Everything is removed from the scene: us, the equipment, the shell of a man. We lift off and fly past the reddening slopes of the mountain, where the marks made in the snow by his crampons and ice axe will now be almost gone. This light on the peaks is referred to as alpenglow – the softening, dying light that hangs on the heights before the blue of night rises up the flanks of the mountain and extinguishes it. Again and again.

Confusion

I lived in the lee of these mountains. The darkness of their storms hung over my town; jagged-edged sunsets bathed us in their glow. The nor-wester blew hard before storms, the mountains were reflected in the lake when it was calm. In many ways, those mountains brought life to those of us living there. Our livelihoods were made from them, we played there at every opportunity, we were connected in many ways; the high snowfields became the river that flowed past close to my house.

My friends, though, were dying in those mountains, doing the same things that I was, and their deaths threw me into confusion. I could divine mistakes in the circumstances of each of their accidents and I could add what I learnt to my knowledge, but I wasn't convinced I could avoid making a mistake myself. The nearness of my escape from the avalanche made it painfully obvious that I wasn't immune to being terminated in the mountains. I felt the pain of their loss on me and others and I didn't know what to do.

In town one day, I walked across the road to the lakefront and sat down on the beach – rounded gravel, cold arse. Across the lake sat the mountains. Consistent heavy snowfalls had draped them deeply over the winter. The snow had brought a grandeur, a presence to the land, but my inherent confusion had kept me away from the mountains, more through a strange inertia than through any definite plan of avoidance.

Despite their distance from me, I had a sense of being in the presence of something powerful, primal and important; call it a 'god' moment. It took me by surprise. I'd had this feeling before in the mountains, but to find it here, safe from their reach, just by looking? That was for other people, the ones in the shops back across the street.

Unsettled, I fretted for a long while. My perception had always been that knowledge came through experience – simple. But with experience came the risk – the very real risk – of dying. I didn't want to be looking but not touching, but neither did I want to die. I could look over the lake to those mountains and know the hazards that existed there – the avalanches, the cold – just as I could feel the reasons for going there – the beauty, the wildness – but part of me felt repulsed by the idea. I couldn't shake it, the feeling that I might now be content just to look, to become a non-mountain person. How could there be meaning without experience? Where would this go?

The winter passed and with the longer days of summer, the usual frustrations rose within me again. I realised that I still needed the mountains in my life; just looking wasn't possible. All I could do was attempt to do things a little differently – in a safer way, I persuaded myself – and choose trips that had different objectives.

As Monty got older, we began cobbling together family journeys into the hills. He saw his first views of the mountains from the comfort of his sheepskin-lined backpack. He loved it, bouncing along on our backs through forests, across rivers and eventually more into the mountains. The trips were a reminder that the mountains weren't all about me, but even this was called into question one day.

❖

It's been some seven years since Monty was up here last. Then, he had been carried up on my back, and Ros's. I'd climbed Mount Brewster in the moonlight before swapping with Ros so that she could do so too. She fed Monty one more time before slipping out of the bag, putting on her boots and shouldering her pack. I wriggled straight into the warm sleeping bag with him, lay out under the stars and both of us went to sleep immediately. Waiting for Ros to return later in the day, we had sat around in the tussocks by the hut, playing together in the alpine sunshine. Seven months old and crawling, he had been intrigued by the grasshoppers, big and fat and able to spring prodigious distances.

Eight years later it's all we can do to keep up. Still twenty minutes away from the top of Mount Armstrong, we are left behind as he scurries off on his own, possessed by some kind of youthful summit fever. Shortly afterwards we come across a couple who are slightly nonplussed to have seen a young boy at the top of a Main Divide peak all on his own.

We're slightly bemused as well, given that only an hour before we witnessed Monty having something of a meltdown on a steeper section of the approach. The fear left him immobile, clawing on his hands and knees, and we had to physically assist him through it. I could see that it wasn't the immediate drop beneath his feet that scared him, but more the sensation of distance – the whispering valley far below, the feeling of being above the world. There were tears and recriminations; we felt we may have pushed him too hard. It was a good reminder that it takes some getting used to, being up here.

On the way down from the summit, we can see Monty's internal excitement, his sheer enthusiasm for being here, especially in the naturalness of his movement, the way he selects a route through terrain. It seems that he was born to use his body like this. Some handy snow patches allow us to show him some glissading and self-arresting skills. He loves the sliding, and why not – he's a child, after all. We session the snow patch, up and down, until we have to call it off in the interests of getting home before dark. We arrive at the bottom of the hill with our older legs quivering and rubbery, Monty badgering us to get a move on, half mocking. We're the ones who have to drive home, though, when he falls asleep instantly in the back seat of the car.

Soon afterwards I was asked, quite directly, 'How do you feel about introducing your child to mountaineering so young? What if, you know, down the track...' The rest of it left unsaid. I didn't understand for a moment what she meant and then suddenly, it all seemed so complicated. Was I really just projecting my desires for Monty onto him? Did I really know nothing better? What if, later in life, he was killed in the mountains – how would I deal with that? I really hadn't thought about it. Shit.

We never really did tracks, not easy ones anyway. Monty found them too boring and we agreed, but it did lead to complications. On our family tramping trips we were snowed into rock bivvies, trapped by floodwaters, bluffed in fog and run out of food. There were meltdowns aplenty and each time Ros and I raised the issue of parental irresponsibility: Is this for him or for us? And what exactly are we teaching him?

Things became more complicated as he grew older and discovered other, more harmful pursuits. The outdoor life was replaced with a less wholesome one. Meltdowns became real anger; words were said, things got broken. There were bad years, and they hurt. It became a wild and bruising ride, but we pulled through – just – and we did so together. Since that time, Monty has done well and has a great deal to be proud of. He doesn't climb much, but he has a strong affinity with the natural world, and it seems that something has rubbed off; even now, he finds walking on tracks boring.

So, introducing him to the mountains? I really don't know, but I do know there are worse things he could have been doing. Perhaps I've dodged that bullet, but everyone needs a guide, however clumsy and well meaning. I'm okay with it.

❖

Despite all the ups and downs of this period, I never completely left the mountains. Every time I saw Aspiring at the head of the valley, there were reminders that it might still be worth it. Changing what I did in the mountains helped too. Ros and I planned a return to the Coxcomb, and decided on a more leisurely style than my normal alpine approach, and to make the most of the situation by taking our time.

Climbing mountains generally requires that you don't dither around, mainly for fear of being caught out in bad weather, but also because there's a satisfaction in moving quickly and efficiently. There are, however, other ways to go about it. We decided we would make the most of our moments away from the usual business of life – of work and childrearing – and bivvy on the route, rather than attempt to complete it in a day. We also decided that we would fly in rather than walk, having reached a stage in life where we had more money and less time, and simply because we could. It seemed a relief to be planning a trip in this style and, as a bonus, there was to be a full moon.

We started pitching lower down on the route than we might normally have done, because without the need to get back down again that day, there was no hurry. The rock was a tad scrappy in places, but happily the steep bits were of excellent quality. As we climbed, I recognised a distinctive rock feature that Rob had belayed off last time and the ledge that I'd fallen asleep on. We passed our abseil point and I found a certain rightness in being there again, some letting go of the sadnesses from last time.

Both of us enjoyed the moderate climbing and especially a beautiful corner up the front of the steep tower that marks the end of the lower rock section. The route above this carried on up a classic snow arête that Ros led in the pink glow of a fine weather sunset, as I paid the rope out and watched the full moon rise over the flatlands of home. The arête ended snug against the headwall of the summit ridge and we spent some time flattening it into a sleeping platform. It was a dramatic place to bivvy, on that high crest of snow where the sun set red and the moon rose at the same time. I remember my lover smiling, at least in part because we were there together and really, what could be better?

The night was a comfortable one and the climbing the next day – via the World's Most Exciting 5-Metre Abseil – was excellent, the rock solid in our hands and the situation spectacular. We traversed the upper Coxcomb along its high ridge of weathered stone, the nearby peaks well below us, with the views raising our eyes further out to the surrounding ranges and further again to the surrounding ocean, only apparent from heights such as this.

We had the luxury of being able to spend a leisurely time on the summit, the area we called home spread out below us. The weather remained fine and there was no real pressure to descend. When we did, it all came together smoothly and we were back at the hut well before the sun had set. The next day a big storm would transform our descent to the valley into a something of an epic, but even that was alright. Things had been put back in place. There had been a return to rightness, for a while at least.

All things change though. Another party, another woman asking difficult questions. I was leaning on the doorframe, trying to keep the weight off my leg and maintain control of my crutches, when she came up to me and said, 'I've known you for ages and you never hurt yourself. What's up with that?'

I knew she was right as soon as she said it: there was much more to this injury. And, deep down, I knew what it was. I'd just never said, not even to myself, that the confusion and doubt in my personal life had manifested itself in this injury. That this accident had been waiting to happen for a while.

I could explain it away and I did, several times, in different ways. The raw facts were that towards the end of a long day's canyoning – too late in the season really, and not in the headspace for a serious trip and running late, I jumped into a pool when I shouldn't have and broke my leg. On the day we were rushing things, which led to the error of judgement, but that wasn't the real reason; when it needed to be, my mind wasn't on the job. I was going too fast, not because the daylight was fading but because I was trying, desperately, to keep on the move in my larger life, to not make a decision I needed to make. I was grasping for distraction.

There was the lingering flavour of a previous dumb idea – the 'losing a girlfriend and soloing something really big in winter' one. There was the same consuming need to be active, to not think too much, to overcome doubt and confusion in my personal life by continuing to do something familiar and rewarding. Only this time it wasn't about salving the pain of a love that someone has lost for you, but avoiding the pain of losing your love for someone else, and not dealing with it very well. So I kept busy, kept active and eventually hurt myself.

Taking off on adventures is easy – stripped down decision-making, close and simple relationships, the delicious touch of oneness with the natural world. The grudging realisation that, much as I'd like it to be, life isn't that much like climbing, took a long time to come. That, unlike the direct simplicity of climbing, real life is complex and compromise is to be found everywhere. Climbing teaches you climbing, adventures teach you adventuring, but they don't resolve your personal issues. The world of the mountains is no real preparation for them. But if it keeps you going for a while, and allows you to ignore the problems, why not stick with the familiar?

On one level, the mountains provide physical and mental space, an opportunity to clear a cluttered mind. The immediate and simple requirements of a low-key trip in the hills provide relief from the constant churning of a confused mind, but the motivations of a big trip can be dangerously different if the object is to provide a distraction. It took me a while to recognise the distinction. Only eventually would I learn to match the sort of trips I did to the way I felt at the time – to respect the notion that there needed to be some nuance in my doings in the hills. I gradually began to understand my motivations better. It still took a broken leg, and for someone to ask how it happened, but it could have been worse.

The local spectacular

Sometimes you can think too much, and even if the things you do are distractions of a sort, they can still be well worth it, at the right time. Of all the distractions I have set up for myself over the years, the greatest have concerned searching out the unexplored which, as far as climbing goes, means new routes. The focus required to attempt something previously unclimbed, engages the draw of the unknown, brings an extra depth of connection to that place, to that feature. There were still things left to do, and it became too hard to stay away for long. Spectacular new routes on the big faces of my home mountains?
Too much to resist.

Although we shared a climbing-based life – he had been an alpine guide for years – and he lived just down the street, I didn't really know Russell that well. One day, however, we were talking about mountain stuff over a neighbourly beer, discussing local options, when the subject of the North-east Face of Aspiring came up. Having put up a route on it with Rich, I recalled the splitter cracks and sharp-edged holds, the excitement of good rock in an untouched place and the wild feel of the far side of the mountain. I also remembered the large unclimbed sweep of rock on the right-hand side of the face and after a couple of beers it was settled – Russ had a few days off and we were going there to put up a new route. So off we went. To make the trip more interesting, Russ suggested that we camp rather than base ourselves at the hut, and it was this little detail in particular that made the trip special. First, I got to know Russ better outside of the hurly-burly of the hut and, second, we got to watch a beautiful sunrise and sunset all on our own, over on the western side of the mountain, where nobody else was.

Despite technically being the north-easterly aspect of the mountain, the North-east Face is very definitely on the wild west side of Aspiring – the side where no one goes. Threading the steep and crevassed slopes on the way around to the bottom of face is a masterclass in crevasse travel. The rope is always tight when it needs to be and Russ makes the route-finding easy. Easy enough that we arrive at the bottom of the route soon after first light, changing from our alpine boots to rock shoes as the wall above us is illuminated in the first light of the day, a smooth and compact sheet of golden stone.

There are no obvious features to show us the way, so we pick a small corner in the middle of the face and just head up, to take on whatever we find along the way. What we find is around 10 pitches of beautiful schist that feels like fine grit sandpaper; absorbing and sustained climbing. We swap leads in an easy rhythm; few words need to be spoken and it seems an easy partnership. The glacier below us rises to the rows and rows of ranges out to the west. As we ascend, the sea comes into view beneath a faultless blue sky holding within it the sun that warms both us and the rock on which we climb.

After several hours, the angle of the face lies back a little and immediately the nature of the climbing changes. The grittiness of the rock allows for an array of loosely stacked blocks to adhere crazily to the surface of the face, steep though it still is. When we look up, it's as though a puzzle has been set for us – a solid slab of stone with randomly positioned counters of precarious blocks, poised and serious and to be avoided at all costs.

'Ropework,' says Russ, 'it's all in the ropework – make sure the rope doesn't catch any of those flakes and we'll be right.' As I set off he offers another piece of advice, with a wry smile: 'Oh, don't pull on them either.'

I find the climbing completely involving, placing runners and manipulating the ropes so they don't catch on the loose bits, weaving

my way on generally solid stone through a maze of precariousness.
I don't normally enjoy loose rock, but I enjoy this. Over the next three
pitches I don't knock anything much off and neither does Russ.

We top out high on the North-east Ridge, back into the sun that had
left us on the last few pitches. It's a long and chossy way up and over
the summit, and a quick few abseils down the flank of the ridge to the
glacier seems the right alternative. We are back at our tent with time
in hand to savour the last of the day. From the ridge behind us we look
down the other side to the Bonar, and can see a couple of other parties
returning from their ascents of the normal route of the North-west
Ridge. There have probably been a dozen ascents of the mountain today
and the hut will have been busy. We woke to no one else and saw no one
else the entire day, and our view to the west holds nothing that isn't the
wild stuff of South Westland. We sit in solitude and toast the sunset.
Russ liked a wee dram.

This climb held an ease of execution and humour that can be
generated only by someone who spent a lot of time in the mountains,
someone who genuinely lived a mountain life. Not many full-time guides
climb recreationally, but Russ didn't seem to be away from home when
he was in the hills; the mountains seemed the place where he was most
alive. Buried by an avalanche high on Mont Blanc in 2016, Russ was 60
and still guiding when the mountains called him in. I imagine he would
think it had all been worth it.

The Kitchener headwall delineates the upthrust massif of Mount
Aspiring/Tititea from the Kitchener Valley. It is a raw and exposed edge
of stone made visible to the world; the face of a major fault exposed for
a distance of several kilometres, rising to its highest point at the right
hand end as the East Face of Popes Nose. The wall, sheer as it is, reveals
the horizontal layers of the world beneath it and these layers run across

its full width, buckled and multicoloured. Each layer has its own flavour, its own character, especially to someone climbing it. Twenty years on, I remember it as if it was yesterday.

Route description for Pagan Poetry, East Face of Popes Nose

Start: Just to the left of centre, below the white patch which is the quartz shield of the fourth pitch, where it doesn't look quite as intimidating as it does over to the right. Watch the morning sunline descend the face above until it is all lit up gold, relish being beneath such an enormous land feature and feel a bit presumptuous.

Pitch 1: A steep blocky sort of crackline with sharp-edged, chunky quartz jugs. Thick veins of quartz zigzag through the rock like spiderwebs. Marvel at how solid the rock is and thrill at the thought of the entire face above being as good as this. The pitch finishes through an overhang and arrives at one of the narrow but flat belay ledges that are a feature throughout the route.

Pitch 2: Is a soft compact green-schist, weathered to a lower angle, the cracks rounded out and hard to protect. The rock isn't quite unreliable but you could scratch your name in it with a piton, if you had one. The climbing is easier, which is good, because it is more run out.

Pitch 3: This kicks up again to vertical. The rock is an even light grey, with a clean architecture of cracks and corners. It has the texture of fine sandpaper and is perfectly solid. From the ledge at the top of this pitch it's necessary to choose between a magnificent right-facing corner, or an even more amazing face crack directly above. We chose the face.

Pitch 4: The shield above is split by an angled crack for pretty much a full rope length. One side of the crack is offset from the other by only a couple of centimetres, but this means a long section of laybacking up the centre of a smooth plate of stone, frosted in micro-quartz crystals extending away on either side. The angle of the sun, now high above the face, ensures the crystals are alight, like fresh snow sparkle. It's hard to imagine a better pitch. At the top is a cramped belay stance, balanced on the upper edge of the giant flake you've just climbed. The situation is very fine.

Pitch 5: This band of stone is purple and pink, a matrix of thin swirly lines imitating the folded layers of stone writ large across the face, and super hard. There's another narrow horizontal ledge at the top and from here the sweep of the face above, and especially the bowl to the right, becomes very apparent; the face is massive.

Note: At this point it's possible to traverse over to the left on a narrow ledge system that widens enough to remove harnesses if you need a toilet stop. There's also a small waterfall to replenish water bottles and wash under. About now the sun leaves the face in shadow and you traverse back again to resume climbing.

Pitch 6: From the right end of the ledge, head up the steep pillar that will take you to the right of some lower angle terrain above. The rock is now a darker, more weathered schist with a variety of features, and it feels reliable to climb on. The scale of the face at this point is impressive: smooth sheets of stone sweeping across the curve of the wall, hanging above long rows of overhangs, falling sheer to the glacier, now far below.

Pitch 7: Starts from a bigger ledge than usual, with some rubble on it. Climb the splitter cracks to the steep pillar. The climbing is on the pillar and the gear is in the cracks, but it all works out. There's something here that looks like guano leaking from a pocket, but it's just some kind of mineral seep. It's too high up, I think, for falcons.

Pitches 8–12: Between each pitch there are now wider ledges, covered in mid-sized boulders and rubble that is generally secure, but care should be taken; the rocks look shifty and it's a long way down. The climbing continues to be fine and the gear solid. The rock is more consistently dark grey, fine-grained and weathered into rounded pockets and wrinkles, rugosities of all sorts, really. The quartz is now present in small flecks and occasional thin seams. The cracks seem to be where intrusions have fallen out of the stone; they're often lined with a fine concreted dusting of quartz.

Finish and descent: The angle of the face eases off and the last section is a bit of a haul up a precarious-looking but mostly stable rubblefield. It's probably best to take the rope off as it will just become an aggravation on the awkward terrain. Top out on the shoulder of the mountain, where the upper edge of the Bonar meets the final pyramid of Popes Nose and marvel at how a mountain so steep, long and difficult on one side, can be so short and mellow on the other.

Search for an anchor amid the choss on the ridge. Settle on the biggest pile of rocks to put a sling around and abseil off it, into the last pink light of sunset. Then spend the night cold and shivering in your bivvy bag, peering out at a bright gibbous moon through the gap left by a broken zip. It may be a sleepless night thanks to both the cold and the rising wind that causes your uncloseable bag to flap noisily.

Start the next day sitting in the lee of some boulders at the top of the wall, touched by the first sun and feeling as though the valley cloud is an ocean lapping at the foot of the great cliff below your feet. Then enjoy a leisurely and hedonistic descent, across the bright flatness of the Bonar, down the spectacular ramp of the Quarterdeck and the leg-burningness of French Ridge, to the verdant valley floor of the Mātukituki. To cap it all off, on the way home, you might be able to sit on the beach at Glendhu Bay and see the face in the distance again, across the smooth evening-still waters of the lake, over the beech-green forest of the valley and above the summer-dirty snow of the glacier, and imagine how it might be to return and attempt another route through the steeper stuff out to the right.

Note: Twenty years on, I'm still imagining the same thing.

❖

I remember the East Face of Popes Nose in winter too, but for different reasons. At some early stage of my climbing career I had come across a half-page ad for some finance company, which I tore from the newspaper. It showed a gleaming ice line up a massive alpine face, glowing in a wild winter sunrise. From the moment I saw that picture, I was sick with longing. The desire it generated turned into a lasting and recurrent illness; an inexplicable cornerstone of my imagination.

When I moved to Wānaka I discovered what the wall was. Other people climbed the face first, but that didn't upset me too much. Before I could even imagine what it was like to climb something like that, it was about 'the direct' – the searing and teardrop-straight line that dropped from the summit. The face was impressive but the line held the key to my heart.

I set about getting to know it. I clambered up various vantage points, at different times of year, to find out what it would need, what it would mean, to climb this thing. It became obvious that everything would need to be just right. The ice on the face formed seldom and formed well even less often. Timing would be everything but that was okay because I would watch it until it was right. Then, one day, it was.

Despite having always wanted to climb it in a purer style, we arrived there, Allan and I, by helicopter, our desire outweighing our ideals. Conditions, however, were perfect. The ice had been burnished into solidity by a winter's worth of spindrift and melt/freeze. The first touches of spring sun had melted it back enough to expose the rock beneath – just enough to provide the reliable protection we needed.

We started at midday, as the sun left the face in shadow and reached the crux as it grew dark, the climbing everything we had hoped it would be. I lowered off from the high point and stayed attached like that all night, just sitting in my sleeping bag, the ropes hanging from the runners above. My dreams were the same as the ones I'd had many times before, the ones that meant I knew what the crux would look like – the approach to the roof, the pull onto the hanging shield of ice, the runout above... It really was like that. It looked just the same.

Arriving back there the next morning, though, I knew within 10 metres, that we needed to leave – immediately. The thin veneer of patchwork ice that laced the rock was starting to disintegrate under the heat of the direct morning sun; we'd left it too late in the season. Small tinkly bits start falling first – warnings – as I looked up at what wasn't going to be. Then, as we abseiled off, tucking ourselves underneath the overhangs, freight trains came roaring past, the face shedding its winter coat. We were lucky to make it down unscathed and walked out, of course, in perfect weather.

It wasn't over. The face was still there, and so was I. Rich and I climbed the route in summer, passing our retreat gear, the rock a marvel, the face feeling friendly. Still I wanted it and still I watched it, my eyes drawn to the wall every time I drove up the valley. The winters passed and I climbed less and less but kept on with climbing ice occasionally, just to keep my hand in so I could have another shot, another day.

Over the next few years there were several more false starts. One attempt ended in an earthquake before we even got to the face. The final one made it onto the face but ground to a halt in crusty conditions, again, only a few metres up the first pitch. Sitting in the snow beneath the face, slumped again in frustration, I realised that I'd had enough. Fifteen years of picturing the positions and pulling the moves, of imagining topping out, of desperately wanting this monstrous thing and it had gone; I had no more to give to the route. I turned toward other realities, I gave it away.

My memory of the winter direct on the East Face of Popes Nose is not one of climbing this most incredible of routes, but rather the mark it has left on me; the wonder of an unfathomable desire and the reality of an unattained dream.

By myself

The scouting trips I had undertaken for Popes Nose had taken me up onto the lower slopes of the East Ridge of Avalanche, in both winter and summer. I bivvied out under the stars, carried only lightweight packs and travelled swiftly over the terrain, eventually making a semi-spontaneous ascent of the ridge itself. I came to love these fast and loose adventures and began to experiment with simplicity. It became easier to walk out the door with a daypack and not much else, and not to have to organise other people.

Conventional wisdom concerning safety in the outdoors, though, holds that you go there with others. Going out on your own demonstrates a lack of understanding about the dangers involved; it's not the way things are done. That helps explain why, especially early on, I'd feel like a naughty child when I headed off by myself. The sense of having to get out the door before someone caught me added to the feeling of anticipation, a trembling like a dog before a walk, that used to come on me when I'd head off into the mountains on my own. It took a while to embrace the feeling.

The other reason for the excitement, of course, was that it could be a whole lot of fun, and I seldom went on a solo mission for which I had any reservations about my motivations. The destination was always somewhere that I wanted to go and it was always my idea, not someone else's, so decisions had a certain clarity. It was all about me and that, sometimes, is a precious thing. I also found a certain relief that no one else was involved, an inbuilt response from years of looking after paying customers, but also perhaps a hangover from the times when my decisions had affected others; the echo, perhaps, of Danny's fall ringing through the years.

When you're by yourself – such a great turn of phrase – there's no one else to blame when your ideas, which often come easily, don't pan out. And there, or thereabouts, lies the truth that solo missions are often safer ones. Alone, you're naturally more careful, more tuned in and less distracted; feeling a little vulnerable brings you to a sensible place quite quickly. The safety factor of having another person is also overstated. Much travel in the mountains, or any adventurous terrain, qualifies as 'slip and you die'. Unless you have a partner holding the other end of a rope, which isn't very often, the other person is no more than someone to raise the alarm, or pick up the pieces – often a reassurance rather than a failsafe.

On a trip to a wild place, it pays to notice everything – you learn a lot on your own. Without the distractions of discourse with others, too, it's easier to get into a flow, that uncluttered space where action manifests in a natural way, unforced. There's more freedom to be spontaneous; the way you move through the mountains, as in life, is purely up to you. Some of the most intense satisfactions of my life have been mine alone. I recommend it.

❖

The best move I ever did was on my own. It was well executed, it was graceful, and it was bold. I guess you'll have to take my word for it.

The head of the Glacier Burn is a big, steep, dramatic place. A large forbidding cliff, dark and water-streaked, wraps around the head of the valley, above which sits the decaying mass of the Avalanche Glacier. The main drainage from the glacier pours over the edge of the cliff in a drop of several hundred metres. Leading up to the waterfall, leaning into it at half-height, a buttress of weathered pink schist ramps up from the valley floor.

I've come to the Glacier Burn for a day trip, and the buttress is calling my name. I scramble up to the place where the top of the ramp nearly butts into the waterfall. From this novel viewpoint, where the rock ends abruptly, it's possible to peer over the edge and visually follow the drop of the fall, all the way from the terminal face of the glacier above, to where it disappears into a gaping black hole in the snow below, snow made from the pulverised ice of debris fallen from the glacier.

Above, the skyline is marked out by the edge of the wall and, in places, angled towers of blue ice.

Down to my right, the severed edge of the ramp falls steeply to the valley and, looking more closely I see that the rock looks magnificent – solid and formed into classic features. I can't help but scramble down to the top of it to peer over the edge and can see straight away that there may be a route down. Not that I'm looking for one – I really don't need to go this way – but that's just what you become in the mountains, a route-finder. Also, I'm not just here to look; I'm here to be part of it.

It feels strange starting at the top of a cliff and climbing down onto it – a reversal of the usual order. The route I've chosen starts with a small left-facing corner, a clean finger crack in the back of the wall. Continuing down this leads to another corner and crack, right-facing this time, and I realise that, without having thought about it too much, I'm climbing on a wall of exquisite stone; that the stone is pink adds an even more exotic air to proceedings. Below me is sheer to the valley, above me is sheer to the sky. The rock is reliable and readable. Moving becomes a pleasure and the route down comes together in a natural way. Although exposed, it doesn't feel wrong.

After some time of concentration and smooth progress, I'm becoming invested in the route continuing – in other words, it's now a long way back up again – when the features I've been following come to an end, and the holds run out into a smooth and featureless slab. Below that the route seems to continue, but I can see no way to get myself there. I hesitate.

The best moves are always instinctive. There is a brief narrowing down to a point, a focus, where the move becomes somehow essential, as does doing it properly. A whole-body memory of moves you've done before visualises the problem, and you forget everything else.

Smearing on slopey footholds and clinging to the last handholds before the blank section, I see, a couple of body lengths directly below me, a pedestal rising from the cliff. It has a flat top about the size of a coffee table. It looks solid. Past the pedestal is air – lots of air.

Releasing the handholds, I slowly pivot on my feet. For one glorious instant, I am standing looking out from the cliff, the valley spread out below me, and in a moment that feels as if the mountains are all suddenly watching, I drop to the pedestal and land perfectly on all fours. The best move I ever did.

We interpret our world through movement. For me, it became one of my main forms of expression, from the dance floor to the mountains. What better way than dancing to realise the infinity of ways to move, and to love that movement without reserve? In the mountains, what better way to understand the slow effects of glaciation than to smear up a polished granite slab, the story of rock formation told through the rugosities your fingers cling to, the freeze/thaw cycle through the changing of snow and ice conditions underfoot throughout your day?

And it's not just what surrounds you. There is also the world within: the aliveness of heaving lungs and aching limbs, the yogic strain of holding a taxing position as you reach for a hold, the uniqueness of each move and the need, at times, to have to put your foot ... just ... there...

Meaning is based on more than just consequence. It contains within it the no-holds-barred joy of physicality and the ability to express it. There's always a marvel in hanging onto the side of some fabulous upthrust of nature – a cliff or mountainside – and even more so in practising the specific types of movement that climbing with a rope allows. There is a particular thrill to moving with the background knowledge that you might fall off but moving on anyway, trusting the rope to save you if you do.

You put the rope on for a practical reason: to be able to climb something harder than you would be comfortable attempting without it. Really, though, it's to involve yourself with the sort of movements – those glorious, limb-stretching, body-twisting, balancey and powerful movements – that exist only in roped climbing or bouldering, where consequence can become secondary to movement, even movement close to your limits, and where you are both limited and energised by the constraints of the terrain.

Climbing with a rope adds a feeling of security, a relaxation that makes it easier to enjoy the climbing. Generally, climbing in the mountains is not so difficult that you're stressed about falling, but hard enough that you're glad the rope is there – a happy medium. But it's those other moments – when you submit to the possibility of falling, but carry on regardless – that stay in the mind. Maintaining mental and physical poise is the essence of climbing. You remember keeping your shit together under pressure, and it feels good.

Climbing without a rope, however, once you get far enough off the ground, is a different thing altogether. Now all that exists is the reality that you can't fall off, ever. This doesn't necessarily cramp your style, but it does direct you towards doing the sort of things you're comfortable with, and to the places where you can make that happen. It seemed a logical progression to me, to move away from harder technical routes toward easier, and ropeless, solo trips in the mountains, where it's possible to climb within your abilities, while still enjoying the sensation of movement.

Technical mountaineering requires that you carry stuff like ropes, rock and ice protection, carabiners – all the jangly, heavy, annoying gear that stays in your pack most of the time, and only comes out for the steepest bits of climbing. Even then, when the gear is clipped onto your harness or hung around your shoulders, it still gets in the way. The times you love that gear – and there are such times – are few and far between.

I don't mind carrying a heavy pack either. There's a certain satisfaction to a hard-fought grind up a long hillside or a tedious slog through breakable snow, a masochistic joy in screaming thigh muscles and a sweaty brow. But it's not conducive to movement, or at least to free-flowing and enjoyable movement.

How does it feel, this climbing without a rope? Well, there's a sense of play – with the space below your feet, the holds in your hand and the bubble of apprehension in your stomach. There is a sense of wonder, balanced with a certain cheekiness that you've made your way to a place like this, along with an appreciation of simplicity. To ensure survival, though, unroped climbing does require the right sort of terrain.

Predictability is what you need. The rock must be sound. There must be a lack of objective hazards, like rock and serac falls. Glaciated approaches aren't advisable. What is good, is rugged. Truly rough country creates a blurring of the lines between climbing and just getting around, and the range of moves you have to come up with widens as the terrain becomes more difficult. Once you learn to enjoy each type of movement, it all becomes climbing. Trips become interesting from start to finish. The thick jungle, the steep vegetated bluffs, the walls and ridges of the peaks themselves, all become part of the climb.

Because steep and interesting terrain encourages competence, skills are developed rapidly, and at some point it should occur to you that one of the main skills you wish to possess is to enjoy what you're doing. Otherwise, what's the point? For me, movement and meaning are almost the same word and they express the same simple thing: the joy of doing my thing, in the mountains. And I now know just the mountains to go to.

PART FOUR

GRANITE

It was Tū-Te-Raki-Whanoa, the famous atua, who, with his great
adze, Te Hamo, shaped the land of Te Waipounamu from the wrecked
waka of Aoraki. He found his last great challenge in the hard stone of
Fiordland. Starting in the south, slowly working his way north and
gaining proficiency with Te Hamo as he went, he perfected his technique,
swinging and hacking at the hull of the waka until the side walls were
breached and the land was flooded by the incoming sea, thus making it
habitable for people.

It was when he moved his attention to Northern Fiordland that he
realised his finest work. Planting his feet firmly on offshore islands,
sliding his hands down the haft of Te Hamo for greater leverage, he
was able to unleash his full powers. His blows created deep and perfect
valleys, the walls smooth and without blemish, the gigantic architecture
of Milford Sound/Piopiotahi and, in particular, the Darran Mountains.
These efforts can still be seen as they were then, the hard stone freshly
hewn, so clean and sheer it's easy to imagine the sweat still drying on
a giant brow.

I love this vision of creation. How life was breathed into the
mountains, how the work of something greater allows people to inhabit
the world, how the land comes alive when people are part of it.

Separated from the folded schists of Otago by the great faultlines of
the Dart and Hollyford rivers, the ancient granites of Fiordland create

an altogether different mountain landscape. Here the hardness of the rock allows the peaks to stand smoothed off and intact, proudly unweathered.

Granite is the rock to which climbers around the world aspire. The steepest and most spectacular peaks of the world's great ranges are granite; it's what you seek out once you've tried out all the rest. It's the same here in Aotearoa/New Zealand. Climbers here have known about the climbing qualities of the Darrans' dark grey diorite for years, the deep pressures of a molten earth made manifest in a rock that, more than any other, has a sense of solidity. Swirls of quartz, flecks of crystals and cooling cracks are inscribed across the vast sheets of exposed slab and in the detail of the holds climbers cling to. The massive walls vary in character, from a smooth compact stone through to a finger-shredding roughness, but always with an enviable reliability. Once I went to the Darrans, I never much felt the need to go anywhere else.

The Darrans – it's a funny sort of name. For a jagged range of upthrust granite to be named after a gentle coal mining valley in the rolling hill country of Wales, almost exactly on the other side of the world, requires a stretch of the imagination. Milford, Pembroke, Cleddau – places of spectacular wildness that are now etched into my psyche – also speak of quiet pastures and stone fences, hand-sheared sheep and country lanes. It's easier to relate to the Māori names of many of the peaks and glaciers, but harder to know their history. Many are named after famous rangatira, but mostly by Europeans.

Right from the beginning, whenever I heard someone speak of the Darrans – the odd person who had actually been there – there was always something, an undercurrent in their voice or a look in their eye, that suggested there was more to these mountains than could be easily divulged.

The weather was an obvious place to start, but then none of

New Zealand's mountain ranges are renowned for their predictable and beneficent conditions. Perhaps it was the rock – a superb granite that was so much better than that further north – but it really wouldn't have to be that great to better the choss found through much of the Southern Alps. It may have been the distance of the Darrans from anywhere, at the end of a long and winding dead-end road through the furthest corner of the South Island. It may have been the rumours of the steepness and size of the walls, the density of the bush or the clouds of sandflies. But then again it may have been rumours and nothing more, just the occasional compelling story from an obscure part of a country that is already an obscure segment of the world. Just some more mountains sticking out of an ocean.

The Darrans seem made for obscurity – concealed by the steep and tortured nature of the land, the rampant thickness of the bush, the rain – buckets of it – cleansing and shaping the landscape, the mist that so often clings close to the saturated ground and wraps around the seeping cliffs. For an explorer, such a place becomes something like the hole in the wall before the rope was there, the place that no one has been to or even seen, the place you just have to go.

Winter

Of all the rumours swirling around the Darrans, the most off-putting, and yet alluring, were the cold ones. Massive avalanches were a popular theme in the mythology. 'Death on a stick' was a commonly expressed opinion about Darrans winter mountaineering, and possibly not an undeserved one. But no one really seemed to know, and among all the fearmongering lay the reality that the small number of routes that had been climbed were real gems, classics of their kind. Even more enticing, most of the Darrans in the 1980s was an unknown quantity, a cold land waiting for people to bring it to life.

Winter climbing revolves around the formation of ice. The Fiordland climate, an amalgam of the maritime and the Arctic, always seems on the cusp of delivering ice, but seldom does. Just as the temperatures drop for a while, a warm front comes in. Just when moisture needs to leak from the snow, frost locks it into place and it never eventuates. There is so much to climb here if the ice is solid, but white means nothing until it's tested with your tools. It is fickle, ephemeral and frustrating. To climb here is to be drawn into a world of esoterica, made up of supposition and voodoo luck; no one never really knows what conditions will be like. Plans are constantly hatched and, on arrival, constantly dashed. For me, the Darrans became irresistible.

On top of all the uncertainty and inconvenience it is also, no doubt, a serious place. Large amounts of snow can fall in a short time, and temperatures can change quickly, creating avalanche conditions that are a constant threat. Many of the obvious routes are big gully lines draining large hanging snowfields, so the potential for being avalanched is obvious. As lines though, they are peerless, impossible to ignore, and I set my sights on them, but it was also obvious they had to be approached at the right time, with the right attitude. Ah yes, the right attitude.

I leave my flat in Dunedin around midnight, getting out of a sleepless bed into the middle of a rainy winter's night, just packing up and driving off. When you gotta go, you gotta go. This coastal easterly will cover the Otago and Southland plains and be backed up onto the edge of the mountains. Over the Divide, it'll be fine; it'll be fine in the Darrans.

The Triumph, despite being a classic car with wood trim features and a three-speed gearbox, has its drawbacks. It had once spent a few days underwater during a flood at Homer and because it never dried out properly, mould grows in the floor carpet and the windows tend to fog up. It also has no stereo and so, with no one else to talk to, I mostly drive listening to my Walkman – my bright yellow Sony sports

Walkman – or just the sound of the car on the road. Road trip noise. Mushroom smells.

I arrive at the Marian Valley carpark in the dark, after hours of driving through the Southland night, mostly at 70 mph, according to the optimistic speedo on the walnut dashboard, the last hour only slightly more sedate on the gravel of the Milford road. There is no other traffic, just possums. The Triumph doesn't have much of a heater so I'm wearing most of my clothes. This means there isn't much else to pack – ice tools, crampons, some food – and remember to get water from the lake. I debate with myself whether to take the Walkman but decide against it; I'll need to save the batteries for the drive home.

The next two hours are a pre-dawn stumble up the track to Lake Marian, following the small pool of light my headlamp throws into the forested night. Dark strands of moss and wet lichens drape the twisted branches of the forest and, as always in the dark, my motivations seem questionable, my movements clumsy and mind full of babble. The bush doesn't help me out.

I exit the forest, arriving at the lake as the light comes quietly to the world, the high white walls at the head of the valley the first to emerge from the night's shadow. There's no sound or movement, just a stillness, a brittle waiting in the air. It's a moment for pausing, here where the track finishes and something else starts. Ahead, the South Faces of Sabre and Marian are a reminder of why I'm here.

The surface of the lake, frozen solid a month ago, has melted back from the edge, which means I'm unable to reach the ice and walk across as I have before. The green depths under the ice look repellent anyway and the thought of breaking through is too much to bear. As I circle the lake, the rough boulders of granite are licked with verglas and I have to concentrate on not slipping. To take in the spectacle of the sunlight, now starting to touch the peaks above, I stop often, but briefly.

Here with the mountain world appearing fresh around me, I start to move more fluidly and to feel better. The outlandishness of my idea

– to solo a new route on the South Face of Barrier – now seems a more natural inclination and from what I can see of the ice conditions up high, I've timed it right. The big faces of Sabre and Marian, dark a month ago, streaked with thin vertical runnels of ice, now look fat and white. It's hard to discern how long ago the last snow has fallen, but I reason that the weather on the coast would only have touched lightly here and there's something about the whiteness up there, some preternatural luminance, that draws me.

The route around the top of the cirque headwall that guards access to the upper Marian is a steep grind from the valley, before leading to an exposed traverse, slick with snow and frost over tussock. I wear my crampons for the added security they offer, stopping frequently to clear them of dirt and vegetation. I rest in the early sun that bathes the end of the traverse, the last I will see before entering the deep trench of the upper valley. From my resting spot I get my first good look at the route I intend to climb, a long twisting gully that takes a line of least resistance up the face.

It looks good. Although the snow underfoot is crusty and unreliable, the steeper whiteness ahead appears glazed and firm, ideal for the security I'm seeking. Anticipation and excitement run through me: no one else has tried to climb this wall in winter. It may be a delusion, but this seems to add an importance to my efforts.

The possibility of delusion becomes more apparent at the bottom of the route. The line, a prominent gully snaking up to the summit, stretches out above me and now, up close, I begin to question the conditions. The whiteness had the look of premium alpine snow-ice, formed by freeze-thaw and the polishing of spindrift, that makes for secure climbing. The snow I am standing in looks like that too, but the reality is very different. A breakable crust covers a strange unbound layer of cold snow, a bridging glaze over looseness; rain crust over powder. I convince myself, though, that up there it will be better. It has to be.

I stop before the main steepening and stamp out a platform to get organised on. Once ready, I start pigeonholing upwards. The snow underfoot requires a good kick each time to anchor my feet. They feel secure, but my axes bite a little too easily into the crust and tend to pull through as I weight them. This isn't ideal but, with care, I can see that the route should be climbable in these conditions. It's not what I want – I want perfection, I want the dream – but there seems little to do but continue, not yet enough reason to retreat.

The climbing becomes more of a struggle, less of an enjoyment. The angle steepens up to around 70 degrees, the point where weight starts to come onto your arms and the security of your tools matters as you start to pull on them. I come to a steeper section, a kind of frosted pillar just a few body lengths long. I stop to rest and draw breath before committing, feeding my resolve.

Just a few moves into the pillar, things fall apart. My feet collapse suddenly in their holds and I'm left hanging on my arms. The picks of my tools lose their bite and start to shear. I strike repeatedly at the crud in front of me, kick and scratch for purchase, but my hacking just makes it worse. I'm now surrounded by nothing but insecurity. It finally occurs to me that this thing – this monstrous thing that suddenly seems to be verging on madness – has come to an end. I hadn't considered it as a possibility but here I am, very far from home, halfway up a mountain, arms buried in rime and unable to move up or down. I feel like laughing even as I feel like crying. So with nowhere else to go, a tiny foolish spot in a frozen whiteness, I start to dig.

It's coming up to midnight – the 24-hour mark – and I'm getting closer to home. Despite the time, there's a light on in the pub in Milton and a pie in the warmer. Washed down with a Coke, it should get me home. It's still raining here on the coast and has been most of the time I've been away. At least I got the weather right.

I slip a tape into the Walkman – Toy Love, loud, brash and fast, just right for the remaining distance. I put on my headphones, turn the volume up to full and watch the speedo rise to the 70mph mark again, all the way home. Home, where the Walkman batteries finally die. Home, where, as I arrive, the red engine light comes on because I've driven the whole way from Milton in second gear, unable to hear the engine screaming over the noise in my headphones. Home. Just home.

I grew up learning that, from a mountaineering perspective, there are two types of danger: objective and subjective. The first are those hazards that actually exist – rocks falling on your head, ice cliffs likewise, and weather changes that create the dangerous conditions that'll get you. Avalanches, for example. Subjective dangers are the ones you bring with you, starting with deciding to go mountaineering in the first place, through the wide range of potential mistakes – tripping, slipping, feeding the rope incorrectly through the belay – to some ultimate bad call that leads to disaster. Within this category I'd put going climbing for the wrong reasons. But what if climbing something big and hard feels like just the thing you need to go and do?

It can be a long hitch from Dunedin to the Darrans, especially in the depths of winter when there's no traffic, and the weather's no good. I'm standing on the outskirts of Mossburn, the first of only two towns on the road to Milford, which is still hours away. The rain is coming down hard and I'm wearing most of my clothing. The rest of my winter climbing gear is in my pack, heavy and getting heavier as the rain soaks into it.

I'm on the roadside by a small cottage and I've been standing there for ages. Smoke issues from the chimney. Fifteen metres from where I stand, there's warmth and dryness, maybe even companionship, although no one has come out to offer this or anything else. Maybe it's because they also have tears streaming down their face; maybe because they, too, have just split up with their girlfriend. Maybe that's why they're playing The Seekers – 'The Carnival is Over' – at full volume, or maybe they're just trying to move me on. I'd love to go but I can't leave, I can't stop listening. It all seems so right.

I sleep the night in a hay barn and it takes the bulk of the next day to get to the Hollyford turn-off. The guy dropping me off there doesn't say anything as I get out of the car, but I imagine he's shaking his head. He leaves me by the barrier arm that signifies that the road is closed, with snow and darkness starting to fall, and disappears without a word. It takes a couple of hours to walk the road up to the hut and by the time I arrive the snow is ankle deep. I've walked in a deep silence to here but the storm is building: the wind is shaking the snow from the trees and there's the sound of avalanches in the heights. There's no one at the hut, there's no one in the valley, there's no one here but me. Perfect.

This place is familiar and I feel at home as I potter around getting comfortable, lighting the fire and the candles, arranging my wet clothes around the place to dry, especially my boots. I can't have wet boots because I've come here to climb and I intend to, as soon as the storm passes. Climb something big.

It's sometime later, after organising the wood, making some dinner on the top of the potbelly and tidying up a little, that I get around to opening the bottle. The storm has progressed markedly. The snow on the ground, already as deep as I've ever seen it, is being thrown around by an increasingly rowdy wind that hits the hut in gusts strong enough to shake the building. There's now a whistling and moaning through the forest all around. Ideal. I settle in.

By the time I'm halfway through the bottle, the storm is raging and through the shrieking of the wind around the hut I can hear the avalanches and sometimes feel a vague tremble in the earth underfoot. It's hard to tell where they're originating but in a storm like this, they'll be everywhere. I imagine the view from up high, looking down on this hut nestled in one of the few remaining patches of forest in the avalanche-scoured valley, tiny beneath the huge cliffs with those giant snowfields sitting – waiting – there above. I wonder then, just for a moment, whether this storm will be the one to take out this hut that for so long has felt like such a haven. But then I turn back to the bottle because when you're getting pissed you just don't care. I start writing a poem in the hut book, about drinking this bottle and how she left me.

There's a scratching at the door. I lurch up to open it and there's a kea standing on the porch. He's wet and covered in snow and when I wedge the door open and stand back, he hops inside. I can tell he's grateful because I've been in this situation myself. I introduce myself, as you do, but Mr Kea is a bird of few words and seems more intent on just warming up by the fire. I resume my position at one end of the couch, he at the other. He doesn't drink. A period of companionable silence follows and by the time he's looking all fluffy and warm again, I've finished my poem and so I read it to him. He likes it and shows his appreciation by starting to hop around and play with the cutlery on the bench.

The bottle is now empty, but there's another. Things are getting more party-like and we're getting on famously when it happens. I think at first it's a lull in the storm, perhaps a brief hiatus in the howling wind, that allows us to hear it, just in the background at first but then louder and louder. Suddenly it's really, really loud and the trees all bend over as one and the wind blast slams into the hut and there's a great roaring and a straining. For a moment we look at each other, Mr Kea and I, and wonder if this is indeed the one.

It isn't, and Mr Kea leaves soon after to check on his family and friends who hang out in the bivvy rocks further up the valley. I go to sleep and wake up cold and distorted on the sofa as the first grey daylight appears. Later investigation will show that the snowfield on the Notch Route on Talbot had gone big – big enough to pile up avalanche debris into the forest and bowl over a few old trees. Not big enough, though, to wipe out the hut.

The walk down the still-closed road the next day, my pack lighter now – what with dry climbing gear and an empty bottle – involved climbing over long sections of piled up avalanche snow. Cloud still hung around the mountain flanks above me, so I couldn't see the route I'd thought to come and climb, not that it made any difference.

Further down the road I met the crew clearing snow and debris from the highway. They were very unimpressed to see me: 'Don't you know how fuckin' dangerous it is up here, mate?'

I assured them that I did. I really did.

The multitude of unclimbed winter routes in the Darrans filled my head. The Triumph eventually died and was replaced by an equally suspect EH Holden. The long drives through the Southland nights got no shorter, or warmer. Eventually, however, there were successes and those glories, when they happened, were once again worth it. Matt and I climbed the huge and unlikely Psychopath Wall above the hut, on one of the few occasions it has ever formed up sufficiently. Its accessibility allowed us to arrive with our bellies full of pancakes, not exhausted and scared from the approach. We adapted to the reality of the strange ice conditions and scratched our way up an ephemeral line, linking patches of every imaginable variation on frozen moisture.

The top few pitches of the route drained the Talbot snowfields, forming a spectacular chandelier of waterfall ice at the very top of the wall. There was true verticality and the ice at last was hard and real, a comforting change from the insecurity of the wall below. Near the top of the crux pillar, arms screaming with effort and hands losing grip on my tools, the runout substantial and spindrift pouring over me, I had a feeling of incredulity that I was there at all, a speck of insignificance amid the unlikeliness. I sank the crucial tool placement over the finishing lip and howled in ecstasy. Briefly, we felt as though we were getting the hang of it.

There was one venue, though, that beckoned beyond all others, and we returned there repeatedly. The South Face of Sabre has everything a proper winter objective needs: a dark foreboding demeanour, a legendary existing route, a difficult approach, a hazardous descent, hard, searing, unmistakable lines.

Brian and I made an attempt on the unclimbed line up the centre of the face. Just getting to and from the route was something of an epic: it took three days to make it as far as the bivvy rock in the upper valley and back. The weather came in and we encountered a life-threatening abseil retreat down the cirque headwall. More than anywhere else we had climbed, the upper Marian had an air of seriousness that never went away.

Allan and I finally climbed the existing route on Sabre, Hongi's Track, along with Brian and Matt. The line, the climbing, the whole damn thing was terrific – big, wild and hard without being too much for us. On the summit we parted ways. Matt and Brian descended the East Ridge, Allan and I the West, which dropped us into an unexpected two-day wilderness adventure and snow plod down to a frozen Lake Adelaide and back over Barrier Knob.

Brian and I wanted more. We returned to again attempt the searing central line. We retreated from low on the route, the ice thin and fragile even though the conditions looked good from below. We tried again later in the season, hoping for fatter ice. Retracing our steps through the cirque headwall and over the avalanche prone approach slopes, we were forced to retreat yet again as our tools once more encountered rime-covered granite. We never really hit our stride. We were always on edge, our vulnerabilities more exposed by the consequential feel of the location. But I remember the climbing, I remember the effort, I remember the fear. And, more than anything, I remember the place.

The big routes on Sabre are still unclimbed, waiting for someone else to put in the effort and feel the lurking fear; probably to climb with new techniques and gear but perhaps to also find, on the first swing of the pick, that what seems, from the bottom, to promise fine-looking snow-ice, is in fact crusty rime that won't hold body weight and that everything here is not quite what it seems.

Some classic climbing was accomplished among all the insecurity, the failed attempts and the driving back and forth from Dunedin. On the lower tier of Cirque Creek, Richard and I found reliable ice, a proud line and a big adventure. 'White as a Sheet', we called it, as much in reference to the pallor of Richard's face after the monster lead fall he took halfway up, as to the smooth and poised sheet of ice we climbed. We were happy. It nearly finished us off, but we took what we could get – another victory of importance only to ourselves – and it felt like plenty.

We discovered other routes on the more reliable lower wall, but our eyes were constantly drawn to the upper tier routes, which could be seen easily from the road. The big and bold gully lines of previous generations were interspersed with the unclimbed, but obvious, routes still to be done, and we finally felt brave enough to try them.

One line in particular stood out. I spent several hours belaying Allan on the initial crux pitch, which turned out to be a barely protectable monster. What had looked from below like a meaningful and consistent flow of water ice was in fact a collection of tiny blobs of ice, embedded in a matrix of insecure rime. Allan did a great job of not falling, but it took time. When I had to follow the pitch, I was frozen to the core, and found it barely survivable. We climbed on, however, past the cyclops-eye cave feature that gave a name to the line we were trying, our courage slowly returning with better ice, until at the end of another two pitches we realised the day was almost finished and we were only a quarter of the way up the wall. Before retreating we looked around; we wouldn't be there again. The atmosphere was breathtaking, the walls steeper, higher and more sheer than anywhere else we had yet been. We shook our heads ruefully, the terrain beyond us for now, our insignificance re-established in retreat; a solid defeat. Finally, I'd had enough. Not of the place – I was just getting started with the Darrans – but of survival as an objective. It was time to replace the insecurity of ice for the solidity of rock, the fears of winter with the pleasures of summer.

The call of the wild

I started with the non-winter Darrans by spending the 1989–90 season at Homer, the Alpine Club hut that is the base for climbing at the southern end of the Darrans. In theory I was the hut warden – collecting fees and maintaining the building – but unless the weather was bad, I was seldom there. I hooked up with whoever came to stay and began by climbing some of the local classics, tentatively at first but with increasing enthusiasm. As I moved through the established routes, I realised there was unclimbed rock everywhere, in all shapes and sizes. I walked up to the bottom of these unclimbed walls and climbed them. I abseiled down the steeper walls, placed bolts if needed and then climbed them; I climbed a lot, slowed down only by the weather.

Non-climbing days were often good for other things, such as scrambling over peaks and exploring the valleys of the Southern Darrans. Failing that, there was plenty of sitting around the potbelly stove in the rain. I wasn't the only one; the stream of climbing colourfuls was constant, but I lived for the fine days. Whichever way I looked, there was plenty to explore, plenty to learn.

Once settled in Wānaka, I found it harder to make the five-hour drive to Homer, especially with work commitments in summer. The Darrans, though, commanded my attention more and more and I fitted them into whatever window I could. The drive became part of the attraction, the empty moonlit highways of Southland providing time to reflect, to savour the space between my different lives.

The Darrans reward the gathering of local knowledge; the learning of access routes and finding of ways. It is a complicated place, and steep too, but I discovered that there was nearly always some kind of passage. I ranged more widely, just to see where I would end up, and came to understand that there were easier routes among the difficult and I enjoyed moving fast as others had before me. I developed a taste for ridges. My arms lost their edge, my legs became more those of a goat and yet my travels demanded that I use my hands, my whole body.

I became less of a climber and more of a traveller, though it was often hard to tell the difference.

This southern end of the Darrans is big country and yet, in the further distance, is somewhere rumoured to be even bigger. Lake Adelaide lies on the edge of this almost mythical part of the Darrans range, which people talked about but never seemed to visit. I traversed the route from Homer to the Adelaide Basin bivvy rocks until I knew every rock, every step, every move; in the rain, in the dark, in the fog. The climbing grew harder, the walls we climbed became bigger, the approaches steeper, and it fulfilled me for a long time, but I always suspected that past the lake there was somewhere bigger and steeper yet.

My explorations then took me to the northern end of the range, to the higher peaks of Tūtoko and Madeleine, and I appreciated even more the scale of these mountains, measured through the effort of muscle and lungs. From the proud heights of these northern peaks, I could see more into the area known, somewhat vaguely, as the Central Darrans. It was a glimpse into temptation, with a strong flavour of the unknown, and I resolved to go there. One day, with another summer nearly over, I realised that I could wait no more. When I got there, I discovered that it really was my kind of thing.

This was another trip that occurred when, emotions taut and frustrations building, I just had to go. The weather had been bad for weeks. According to the forecast it looked like staying that way too, apart from the next day or two. I went anyway. 'The call of the wild', an ex-girlfriend had generously called it, when I'd left.

By the mid-1990s I still hadn't been into the Central Darrans, but I'd glimpsed parts of it from high on Tūtoko. When I'd peered into the Lake Turner Basin and the evocatively named Cleft and Chasm creeks, the word Shangri-la was immediately etched into my mind. I'd seen giant

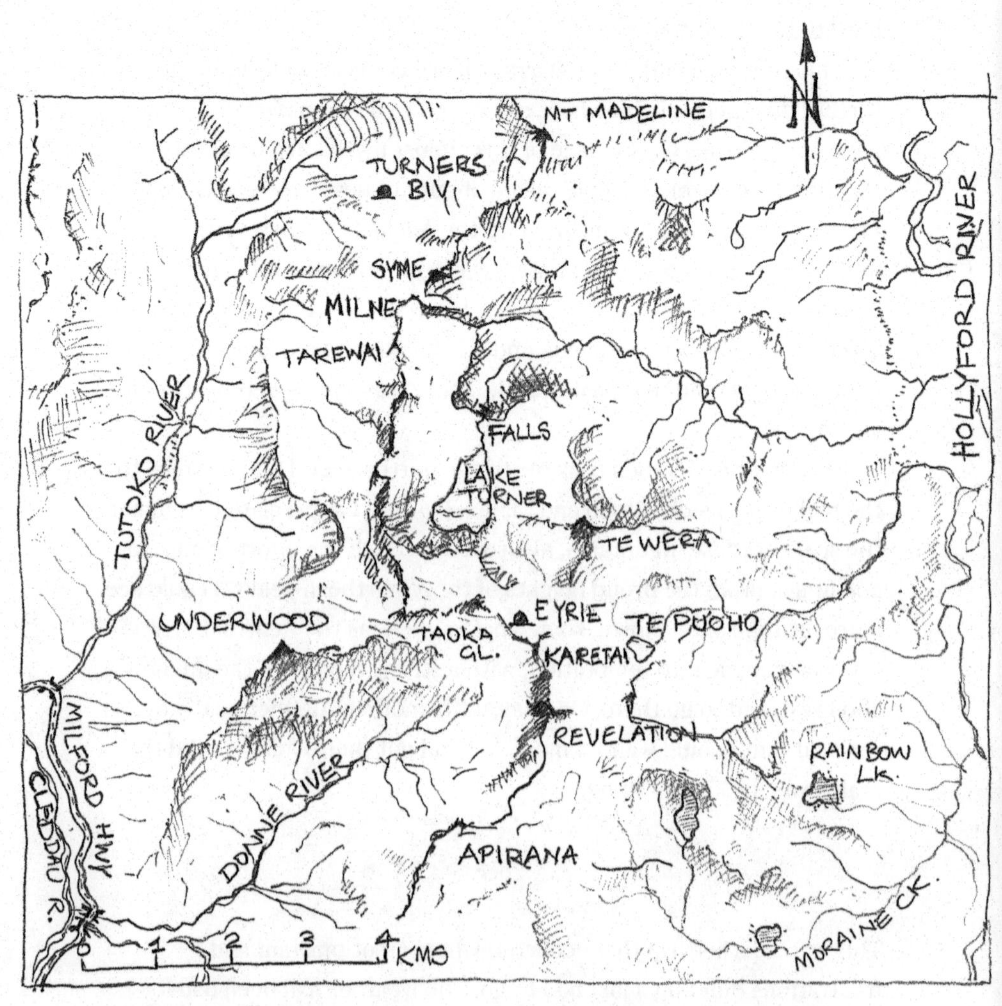

CENTRAL DARRANS

waterfalls, dark alpine lakes and sheer walls with no names. A dizzying rift split the mountains in two, and there were enormous features I'd never heard of. It had grown in my imagination into some mountainous heart of darkness, a blank on the map of my life that needed to be filled in.

What was known as the tree avalanche route on Mount Underwood seemed to me an obvious way to approach the western side of the Darrans. Here a striking line of exposed bedrock provides a vegetation-free super-highway through the jungle, all the way from the Milford road to the tops, without having to get too involved with the surrounding Fiordland bush. By the time I finally got there, though – about two years too late – the moss had grown. Moss holds water, and on this particular morning, that water was frozen and even the cleaner, moss-free slabs had runnels and sheets of verglas iced onto them. It was slick.

April, really a bit too late for this sort of thing, is also a time of shorter days on top of the cold and wet, so I'd started early. The easy-looking slabs were tenuous and slippery and my fingers lost their feeling. It took much longer to scale them than I'd imagined and it wasn't nearly as much fun as I'd hoped. Above the initial steep section, however, where the avalanche had carved its path through a forested bench, several kākā frolicked in the treetops, answering my clumsy kākā noises with rowdy good humour, and cheering me up.

A long upwards haul followed. Underwood is, in a Darrans kind of way – the kind that sees you start at 49 feet (15 metres) above sea level, according to the old Tūtoko River sign – a big mountain. I'd managed to avoid the usual bush bash by using the slip, but the constant bluffs, after the initial excitement, were dragging on. Almost 2000 vertical metres on, and I felt a tad jaded by the time I crested the ridge to find a possum expired and desiccated among the rocks. I empathised.

Many 'real' New Zealand mountains only get started around 2000 metres, but most fail to muster the ambience of the ones in Fiordland. Looking up the Tūtoko Valley from my position, I took in the

unbroken sheerness of the valley walls and could see one of the reasons
for this: the crux of a mountain route here is often the approach.
Getting off your peak and home again involves steepness and effort.
Commitment will be part of the game.

Not to mention that 2000 metres is a long way. I still had a ridge to
traverse to the top, and the summit ridgeline of Underwood is a sharp
one. As you traverse along it, the exposure is tangible: 2000 metres
down both ways, the shady side of the Donne Valley looking particularly
void-like. An unpleasant traverse on loose blocks took me out over the
drop and I emerged from the shade hoping for a more relaxing section.
My view along the ridge was blocked by a striking blade of granite, a
jutting fin poised vertically above the divide. It looked quite easy to
scramble around but I dropped my pack and climbed it head-on, before
I could think about it. It's often best to catch yourself unawares like
that, and I felt completely refreshed when, soon after, I approached the
summit, a bubble of naughty joy lodged large in my chest.

The summit of Underwood is made of magnificent stone, an igneous
mother rock of massive solidity. Its rounded height is a fantastic vantage
point and I settled down to orient myself and work out a strategy. It was
here that I discovered I had no map. I had given up on compasses long
ago in the Darrans, direction being mostly dictated by the difficulty
of the terrain here. A map, however, is a different story. In particular,
maps have contour lines on them, and steepness is critical to the ability
to get around. Tiny contour squiggles might indicate a ledge system or
a faultline, often the only way to progress. Maps also suggest how you
might be able to escape – which valley you may be able to descend in
the rain, which ones gorge out.

There is a certain stage on a trip, when whatever you've wanted to
leave behind, whatever frustrations you may harbour, finally fall away
and things become simple. I love the arrival of that immersion in what
you're doing and in the place around you; of tuning in, of calm. This
happened to me early on this trip, there on the summit of Underwood
with no map.

My bivvy site is beautiful that evening. I sit on ancient wrinkled stone weathered to a burnt orange, similar to the colour of the sun setting over it. Puddles in the rock skin seem as irregular windows that perfectly reflect small pieces of the sky. I can see out over the sea, to the cloud masses above the Tasman. It's hard to pick what shape those clouds may take tomorrow, hard to pick the shape of the day itself. I put on all my clothes to sleep, as the lightweight traveller must, and burrow into my new bivvy bag.

The night is a cold one. I sleep badly and wake up to a frosty coating on the bivvy bag, with the inside drenched in condensation. It seems that my new purchase is rubbish. I have to chip away a solid freeze from the puddles to get water for the morning brew. As I clean up before leaving, I see coffee grounds and garlic peel scattered on the ground and it seems somehow shocking, as if I'm dirty and the world is pure, which is, I suppose, some kind of truth here.

Overnight, I have formulated a plan: keep going and see what happens. I'm not sure what direction this will take, and I digress for some time, peering over the great wall that drops from the north side of Underwood, a dizzying vertical world that ends in the jungles of the Tūtoko Valley. From the edge, I feel the familiar urge to jump, a recurring and luckily rhetorical notion that often takes flight in my imagination. I keep it there and instead wander in sunshine among glorious crags and over wondrous polished slabs. I scramble over stone such as I've never seen before, patterned and firm under my hands, and find a blue ice cave and rest in it awhile.

By late morning I arrive at the saddle above the Taoka Icefall. It seems like a gateway, and instantly I want to go that way. I cross the glacier, so elegantly poised between the yawning depths of the Donne Valley and the dark ramparts of Patuki's South Face. On the right the icefield curves white and broken towards the valley in ever-increasing chaos, before disappearing abruptly from sight. On the left, twisted columns of dark stone rise up into cloud.

Cloud. After crossing the snow of the Taoka, I arrive at the col above the Lake Turner Basin and feel as though I want to stay. I consider heading down to the tussock flats and ruffled water below, the lake evoking feelings of contentment and rest, but the weather is on the change and the lightweight traveller can't afford to sit around waiting for storms; I need to start planning my escape. My somewhat unfocused intention to proceed north would have meant heading into the weather, but without any route knowledge in any direction, I decide to head south, away from the building clouds.

This is one of those moments that events may turn on and I know it's not a choice to be taken lightly. Travelling south will mean traversing over Karetai, one of the sharper and higher upthrusts of the Central Darrans. This in itself seems pretty exciting, especially since I haven't brought a rope. There will be no protection for a tricky section and no way to abseil something I can't climb down. I'm already in a state of relying on instinct as much as rational thought and my decision, really, comes down to a kind of faith – faith that the terrain will be manageable, faith that it will all work out, faith in my ability.

A young chamois keeps pace with me most of the way up Karetai, curious yet maintaining her distance. She's never seen anything like me before. The summit area of Karetai is a chaotic jumble of large blocks, culminating in a massive wedge atop which is, however unlikely, a bivvy. Or rather, four rough walls amid the rubble of the summit, walls that I hope had something to cover them on the night it was used. This rude shelter spoke of achievement. Whoever built those walls had summited after completing a climb on Karetai, probably a first ascent, almost certainly an adventure. Facing the reality of an approaching storm, I can only shudder at the prospect of hunkering down here. A more exposed place is hard to imagine, and I scurry on towards an adventure of my own.

A giant fissure splits the top of Karetai and runs the length of the South Ridge, dividing it in two. The way down begins here and I'm astonished to be scrambling through a tunnel, as if two mountains are leaning against each other. I stop and assess the bivvy options if the down climb doesn't go. Cold air sighs through the walls of the fault and moisture drips everywhere. It may be out of any rain but it has a chilly feel – best to move on.

The tunnel opens to form an icy gut, the bottom of which drops into a dark cleft. I strap on my crampons, tightly. It doesn't look promising. The ice is hard and the situation oppressive as I crampon tentatively downwards. As I near the end of the ice I see that the gully rolls over into obvious impossibility and for some respite I traverse out to the buttress on the side. Once there however, I see that the buttress steepens off below me and also looks unlikely. I stop on a ledge, take off my pack and sit down to relax and absorb some sense of place.

Sometimes the only way to find a route is to take every lead to the end, to ensure that you don't miss anything. Difficult route-finding often comes to this: a narrowing of options until there's just one left. It's important to be thorough and not miss anything, because the prospects of having to move to plan B are almost always worse. In this case, even if there is one, it will involve climbing back up the icy gully, a lot of unknown ground and doubtless a bunch of other dramas. I get up and start looking.

The descent comes together in bits and pieces. A smeary traverse above a big drop is followed by a crack system which, bulge by bulge, takes me down towards the snow. I return to my pack and rehearse the airy moves across the slab a couple of times without it before setting off. At the end of the rock I feel pretty chuffed and am keen to get onto the snowfield. I am forced, however, to wobble around on a sloping ledge to get my crampons back on and impatience, in the form of cursing and fumbling, gets the better of me before I can jump across the 'schrund. Once there, I start running, unable to contain myself and needing some release from having to be constantly careful. I take off along a ridge of firm rough rock towards Revelation, right along the upper edge of the enormous Donne Face. Upwellings of cloud pour up, curl and fall over the ridge. I revel in the exposure and the physicality of it, on all fours often, going flat out. I arrive at the summit of Revelation heaving and shaking with an exultant wildness, matching the building storm. I seem to be answering the call.

On the summit there is a new outlook, and the need for a new plan. When I look back to the north, the cloudscape and landscape now seem one. Boiling masses of cloud writhe through jagged peaks; long fingers reach down gullies; wide roiling walls push skywards. There is wonder being in a wild place in a building storm. You know you're about to be made small and that soon there'll be a period of containment, of hunkering down. Not a loss of control, but a loss of options.

But not yet. A feeling of looming turmoil chases me down the ridge away from the clouds. There's a loose rock section and another ice section, where my crampons hardly mark the blue hardness and want to twist off my shoes. Back on the firm rock above the Korako Glacier, I start to run, the terrain easier now. I come off the ridge onto buckled slabs as the light fades, knowing that I'll be stopping at the first flat spot, at the first place I may be able to find some shelter.

There's no shelter but I do find the only flat spot – a coffin-shaped plinth in the middle of a large depression carved from the bedrock of the Korako Cirque. The term mortuary slab springs to mind as I set my sleeping hovel on it, but only in jest, because I'm enjoying myself. Knowing you're about to get a pasting and that it's well beyond your control makes things simpler. Worry disappears, acceptance is the only reality. I cook dinner in calmness, the breath of the incoming westerly swirling above me for now. The dark walls above me are backlit by a starry sky. Feeling that the weather might hold off a while, I crawl into my pit unconcerned.

The rain starts around midnight and within the hour has become heavy. Being in a bivvy bag is a strange mix of shelter and exposure: the rain is almost on your skin, yet your skin is dry. Noisy, yet removed. The new bivvy bag seems to be keeping the rain out and I feel quite snug and relaxed until I hear a different sound – the lapping of water.

I snap into the realisation of where I am – on a rock in the middle of a no longer empty pool. I crack the zip and the torchlight confirms imminent disaster. I strip off my clothes, roll the whole lot up into a bundle and wade out of the pool. The storm lashes my nakedness as I hunt for somewhere that will work. Every surface is running with water, the wind now strong enough to be picking it up and throwing it everywhere in a fury of wetness. I choose the top of a rounded bulge as the driest spot and re-enter my bivvy world, struggling with the absurd antics of getting dressed within the bag.

I'm forced to sit on my little dome, arms around legs to minimise contact with the water-swept granite, for several hours. At some stage the sound of the rain on the nylon changes to a sharper, harder kind of percussion and then softness – hail, then snow. As with all grim bivvies, the night is a long one.

When the light does come though, I'm still dry. My new bivvy bag has saved the day. I am fully fed, clothed and psyched when I re-enter a grey, miserable world. The rain has returned after the snow and a strange half-glazed mush covers the ground. Each hollow is filled with a soft treacherous verglas. I shove all my gear into the pack and set off into increasingly torrential rain, before I've even woken properly. I need to either find proper shelter or make it down, and I need to keep moving all the time until I do. I head down, determined to find my way through this strange and gloomy waterworld.

It isn't really the conditions that cause me to fall, more a lack of adjustment to my new reality, and it takes me some time to realise that I have. A quick slip, a sharp crack on the back of the head and the world sways as I go to ground. The rain on my upturned face then seems urgent, a reminder that I'm not to lie there any longer, that I must get up and get going. A period of travel passes before it occurs to me that there's been some kind of event, but that it's alright now and I need to continue. For the next few hours I have the sensation of observing my own actions from somewhere nearby, a kind of companion to myself.

The Korako Ledges are a known, if seldom travelled route linking Moraine Creek with the Te Puoho Glacier. I'd heard my friend Murray speak of the alternative ways to traverse the ledges – the high and low options. Looking across now, I can see nothing that looks like ledges and little in the way of options. I don't know where I'm heading and the terrain looks uniformly steep, and wildly storm lashed. As I traverse I keep coming to sudden watercourses, which force me to cast up and down until a crossing can be found. Unbelievably, the rain seems to be even harder and the water in these gullies is gaining ferocity.

The largest streamway forces me down towards the bottom of the ledges and I find myself right on the top edge of the massive overhanging cliffs that drop into Moraine Creek. From its carved granite groove, a jet-stream of water spews out horizontally, curving over and falling free towards the misted forest tops below. The crossing narrows down to one option: a jump only a couple of slippery metres from the edge, the results of a mistake all too obvious. One movement decision among hundreds on the day, but one I can still remember very clearly.

Through the sheets of rain, I can see before me the steep hanging buttress that cuts off the end of the ledges, the cliff-line rising into the dark moisture mass that is now the sky. I need to get over this ridge to make it into the head of Moraine Creek, but have no knowledge of where to cross. Conditions demand that I find the right way the first time, so I resolve to traverse along to the bottom of the ridge and then climb it until I find the route. This means I have to go low, at times almost on the lip of the void below my feet.

I am now as wet as the world around me. I've seldom been in a place that felt so big and dangerous. Everything is water and massiveness and absurdity that I should be here, an insect crawling across a chaotic landscape. The sense of detachment continues, maybe as a mechanism for coping with the overwhelming battering of my senses, or perhaps as some clinical part of me stepping back and taking charge. And somehow, enjoying it.

As I climb onto the buttress, I experience a kind of waking up, as though someone is leaving me to it, with the reality of the situation in my face and under my fingernails. Conditions become awful as the terrain steepens, the snowgrass now so waterlogged that it tears out in heavy sodden chunks or collapses underfoot. Increasingly I'm forced onto the water-streaming rock – a daunting prospect but the place where things finally change for the better. Right on the front of the buttress, a wrinkled prow of granite provides the gritty reliability I need, grip among the insecure slipperiness of plants. The rain hammers down in a heavy squall as I climb through it, unlikely and persistent, to an easing of the angle and the remains of an old cairn – the crossing place I've been looking for.

Once back on terrain with signs of previous travel to follow, I can stop focusing on the moment, and I find already a sense, not of retrospective enjoyment, but of being in the soaking and steamy present, every sense alive. The wet-chill of clothes and skin, the smell of saturated earth and body heat, the quiver of physicality and hunger all feels like a success, a coming-through, and as if in recognition of something passing, the rain starts to ease slightly.

I drop down a steep gully on steps worn from previous parties and enter the head of Moraine Creek. As I descend into the basin my view opens out and it feels as if I've stepped back into another, prehistoric time. There's greenery now – shiny ferns and bloated mosses. Massive waterfalls drop everywhere out of a heavy cloud-base and the valley is filled with mist. It seems primeval, as if flying reptiles should come shrieking from the cliffs and the deluge is a creationist flood. I feel smaller than ever as I traverse back under the cliffs I've so recently been on top of. The rain has lessened but the mountains are still shedding rivers from above. Within its vertical walls the valley roars, alive with a vast energy.

I come to the run-off from the main watercourse, the one I'd had to jump over above. The streamway gouges its way through a steep boulder field and its shifting, rolling bed is alive with the crack and grumble of fast-tumbling rocks. I could wait for it to go down but instead I run and stumble across on a downstream angle, stones rolling out underfoot and always on the verge of going in.

After this I walk with the water, which flows down channels through the tussock and shrubs, and into the forest. The change to a track and my soaking wetness persuades me to start running again, real body cold only a short stop away. As I descend, the skies roll back to a quick and chill southerly clearance, the herald of an ending. When I'm hitching back to my car later that day, one of the road workers who picks me up will tell me, 'Inch an hour for twelve hours, mate', and it means something to me, relating the world I've left to the one I'm returning to.

But as I trot down Moraine Creek, as the skies clear above me and before there are roads and people, there remains a sense only of simplicity, of having, simply, survived. No heart of darkness, no call of the wild. Not for now.

The place that we go

This first solo trip opened my eyes to the potential around Lake Turner and it didn't take much to persuade the Richards that we should go there. Although the area had been visited throughout the previous decades by the occasional group of enthusiasts, little had been climbed in more recent years – certainly not the steeper faces. When we got there, it was apparent that we'd rediscovered the best alpine rock in the country and our visits became a regular feature around which our outdoor lives revolved.

Getting there, with enough gear to climb and survive, wasn't easy. The national park regulations forbade helicopter access and the terrain – high-volume rivers, deep gorges, steep valleys – was difficult with a heavy pack. On an early trip Rich and I discovered a small cave and the concept took shape of having a fixed base in the heart of the Darrans. We could leave our gear there, and shuttle in and out with manageable packs. It was a stroke of genius, and it set us up on a journey that would carry on for years. This is the story of an early trip to the Eyrie, the place that changed everything.

This trip begins, as others have before it, with a dance floor, though this one is surrounded by an entire campground filled with friends and family. The opening ceremony has remembered our friends who have died over the last few years, young and in the mountains, and reminded us why we're here: to come together and celebrate our lives in a positive way, rather than just congregating at funerals. It turns out to be a good idea, a weekend-long outpouring of frivolity and dress-up mayhem, offered up as a suitable send-off for those who are missing.

The next day, the Richards and I leave the clean-up crew to it and head towards the Darrans. The realities of shopping in the supermarket and dealing with 'normal' people are difficult, and we're relieved to get in the car and start driving. With no pressure to get anywhere but Homer, we arrive after dark, savouring the slow transition to the mountains.

It's raining when we arrive, but the hut is warm and dry, although a renovation shambles. We chat with the builders before sweeping aside ankle-deep sawdust and retiring to newly made bunks that are too close to the ceiling to sit up in, a measuring mistake that seems to have been glossed over. This all adds to the childish humour being generated by our enthusiasm for the upcoming adventures. Mark and Tom, also post party and poised on the brink of a Darrans fine spell, are similarly giggly. We wake in the morning with the objective of making our way up a valley none of us have been into before, the Donne. None of us knows anyone who has been there; all we have are the rumours of difficulty.

At first, the track is pleasant travel, and when the route deviates up a side valley, the plunge into greenery is initially daunting. After only 50 metres of bush bashing, though, we're into it. Once we're in the forest, travel is generally acceptable and there's always a branch flicking back in someone's face or a boot going through a rotten log to maintain morale. We deviate to an open and sunny lunch site below Darran Pass, where an avalanche path has cut a swathe of tussock and rock slabs down into the valley. The scale and dynamic nature of the terrain starts to become apparent.

After lunch we shortcut it over a steep tangled moraine wall, which takes us into thick zones of bush lawyer and other vegetative density. It's quite a while later that we arrive back near the river with its easier travel, and some clearings allow us our first views of the steep walls above. The upper valley is big. There's a sense that we've come to a place where meaningful things happen. We breathe deeply the air of anticipation.

The first fantastic thing to happen is the ice caves. Deep and long-lasting avalanche debris, fallen from the hanging snowfields on Underwood, have been carved into a maze of scalloped tunnels, interconnected, blue and echoing. We run around in these dripping caverns for quite a while, a wildness slowly taking root in us. Shortly afterwards we camp on an elevated flat spot, in grass that looks as though the croquet club had just forgotten to mow it this week. Our view down the valley looks deep into Fiordland and although the road is only just down there somewhere, we've already left it well behind.

We light a small 'bushline' fire that night, with small twigs and dry tussock. Surrounded by immensity, it's easy to reverse the image and imagine looking down on its tiny twinkle from above. A thin moon sets perfectly between huge walls that are just darker than the sky. A rogue breeze blows Richard's sleeping pad into the fire, which doesn't seem to matter, even to Richard. The next fantastic thing that happens is that we wake up in the morning and are still here.

Our main aim is to find a feasible access route into Lake Turner and then to occupy a potential bivvy cave we'd discovered. From there, we'll do whatever we fancy for a few days before finding another, as yet undetermined way out; an exploratory foray with nothing much in the way of technicalities. Well, that's what I think we're up to anyway. Rich's vision is: into the bivvy, climb a couple of new routes including our current nemesis (an arête feature of striking magnificence), pick up all our various stashes of gear and call it a day at Lake Turner; in short, a mopping up operation. Richard's motivations are somewhat less complex: he's just along for a good time. As it turns out, this is pretty much the strategy we follow.

Access up the Donne is described in the old Darrans guide as a packing route. It fails, however, to mention that no one has been up this way for decades, due to major recession of the Taoka Icefall, around and through which the route goes, or went. The Taoka stretches all the way across the upper shelf of the Donne in a continuously broken front face, looming over the ice-polished slabs below, which curve over into the valley depths. The icefall behind is torturous, guarding the access gateways of the high cols. On a previous trip, though, I had peered down on this arena and mentally put together a route that wove around and through the icefall. Memory (not my strong point), and an armchair optimism, have me convinced that the route is a good one, and I've persuaded the others to attempt it.

When we get there, though, the view from below looks very different. As we look up from the slabs below the icefall, our entire horizon is a surreal complex of twisted blue ice. The scale of our new world makes us unsure if we're even safe where we stand and we scuttle crab-like across buckled sheets of granite, ever glancing up. The glacier above is quiet so far. At the end of summer, there seems no great load on the ice, which is freezing in and waiting for winter. Nothing moves except us, but increasingly it feels the wrong thing to be doing, the wrong place to be. We stop before the crux of our imagined route – an obviously threatened gully, worn smooth by a constant rushing stream, ice blocks wedged in the narrows. Time is spent casting around, momentum stalls. This, the only feasible-looking route, will not go.

A strange juju runs through our veins as we regain the safety of a shallow buttress. A feeling of relief and correct decisions made is tempered by the real possibility of having to go down – all the way down. We stop and snack, allowing tension to drain, humour to be restored and empathy with our situation to grow.

The chaos of the icefall changes at the Karetai end, where a sheer ice face rises to the flat relief of the glacier above. It's 60 metres high and perfectly vertical, but when Rich says, 'I reckon we could scamper up that', Richard and I both nod our heads. After considering the realities of our single ice axe, hiking shoe and strap-on crampon set-up, Rich then says, 'Or we could climb the rock next to it.'

It all falls instantly into place. We nervously enter the blue shade under the ice cliff which, although stable and old, is not a place where we can relax. As we climb a short pitch on quality rock, we're able to look deep into the melted-out front face – a laughable climbing prospect. We emerge into sunshine, spectacularly poised on the edge of Karetai's West Face. Visually retracing our steps, we see we have pioneered, in the most roundabout way, the simplest, safest and most obvious route. It may not always be so.

Many large blocks lie scattered around the top of the cliff and so, with a sense of boyish elation, we set about tidying up a little. Resonant, booming echoes and the waft of cordite drift over us as we dance around, gleefully pushing random boulders over the cliff edge, shrieking in the sunlight.

After lunch, we crunch across the glacier, strongly fortified with a real satisfaction. There's a 'Mr Explorer Douglas' thrill in working a new route out of a valley system; no contrived line just next to another, no cluttered jangle of gear around our necks, just the easiest way through some difficult country.

The short scramble up to Patuki Col brings us to the edge of the Lake Turner basin. I recall our first trip here, a few short years ago, and the sense of coming home for the first time, of looking up from the lake outlet and being surrounded by grandeur. The best alpine rock walls

in Aotearoa, all unclimbed, seemingly all ours, and so it has been since.
And here we were again.

After we've scrambled up from the col, there's an air of expectancy as
we approach the cave, which we'd stumbled on one day during our last
trip, while fooling around on Karetai. Rich had looked at me strangely
a while back when he'd heard me extolling its size and weatherproof
qualities. Memory and optimism had created a vision of a spacious and
spectacular dwelling among the cliffs.

Some delicate manoeuvres down an exposed gully, across a narrow
ledge system and we're there. Not quite a ballroom, but the situation
is incredible. Rich and I had promiscuously named it Turner's Eyrie,
but eyrie is the perfect description. The lake is spread out far below,
reflecting Tūtoko, Madeleine and myriad other peaks. Further along
the ledge, water splashes over sun-warmed rock. Almost anywhere a
misstep could lead to your doom. We feel like eagles.

We spend the evening feathering our nest. A fine gravel floor
responds well to levelling out, rock walls take shape. We sleep content.
At sunrise, I'm halfway to the lake outlet, retrieving gear stashed there
on a previous trip. A chamois is silhouetted above me against a backdrop
of red snow, red rock, red sky. The stash has survived well under its
rock for two years, the main casualties being the cream cheese and the
inside of my rock shoes, which look remarkably similar.

Back at the Eyrie, the Richards have been beavering away further
into the cave. When we meet at the base of our intended route, they
seem more excited about the new sleeping area than the expanse of
gorgeous red granite rising above us. This doesn't last long, of course.
These are my first rope lengths for a couple of years and, almost to
my surprise, I enjoy the return. The rock feels ancient, weathered and
wrinkled. Our fingertips wear down quickly. We climb six pitches,
all boomers, before topping out onto the North Ridge of Karetai.
The warmth of the late sun soaks our west-facing wall. Our continuing

glee decides us on the scenic route back home via Lindsays Ledges, a narrow and spectacular accessway that cuts across the cliffs opposite the Eyrie. We feel particularly sprightly with our light packs but are still no match for our chamois cousins and it's after dark when we make it back to our nest.

The next morning we're more in the mood to loaf around and so it's officially declared a rest day. A light mist hangs around, somehow reinforcing our decision; there's talk of going for a walk later. 'Later' finds us on the summit of Karetai. The North Ridge is pretty much our backyard now and the rough blocks and gendarmes become a playground. Jumps across gaps, tunnels to wriggle through, arêtes to climb – we are filled with a cheeky, reckless joy.

This energy takes a more concrete form for me when I see the gendarme on the South Ridge rising through the mist; it's somewhere I've always wanted to go. This feature is a massive tower of stone separated from the bulk of the ridge by a gap that's but a step across – but what a step. A half-hour down climb and some intense concentration gets me to the spire, where I look up to see the Richards peering down on me from an equally spectacular pinnacle. Below us it's 1500 metres down to the Donne, where one day these rocks will lie in pieces. Our feet tingle. The afternoon back at the Eyrie passes in a contemplation and readings from the latest *New Idea*, brought in specifically to keep up with the gossip. While Brad and Angelina plan for their baby, we rustle up plans for tomorrow.

In the morning a sense of purpose ripples between us: gear is sorted, lunches are made and headlamps packed. The snow slopes below the arête have collapsed dramatically since our last visit two years ago and we're now faced with more objective hazards in order to access the route. A 50-metre dash under the glacier tongue seems a quick thrill until a deep rumble sounds from the depths, just as Richard is standing under it. Time pauses for a second, even as it stretches and warps through the range of awful possibilities in our minds. Richard stops, raises his hand in a 'halt right there' kind of pose, facing the ice cliff down. The rumbling stops and the ice doesn't go any further, which quickly restores humour, although a faint edginess lingers on.

I hog the easy first pitch and find it disturbingly difficult. Richard then puts in a strong lead to our previous high point. This also feels difficult. We climb all over each other at a cramped hanging stance before Rich sets off into new ground. As he tries to piece together the puzzle above, Richard and I hang on the belay, noticing for the first time that all its components are wedged behind the same enormous block embedded in the cliff, which adds to the general unease. Richard lowers off and we all hang on the belay, looking at the gear. I have another half-hearted attempt before likewise backing off. We mutter about placing some bolts, but only in jest. We abseil off, again. In the after-match debrief we agree: flag the direct start, go for the easier way out left... And so the next trip is already seeded; each time we come back with more projects than when we arrived.

Back on the ground, disappointment quickly becomes a perfectly acceptable state of affairs. A lakeside lunch stop seems every bit as appetising as clawing our way up some hostile piece of rock. The pleasure we have in just being here sustains our keenness and when the idea of heading home the long way is mooted, we're unanimous in our enthusiasm.

The high-level circumnavigation of the lake is something we've considered before and its novelty now seems quite appealing. The route involves a linkage of narrow ledge systems, far above the depths of the lake, and we revel in the slabby travel, our shoes extra grippy on the roughened skin of granite. We look up towards the Eyrie, a tiny dot in the rugged flank of Karetai, and marvel at its placement.

As we start traversing, a family group of chamois strolls back below us. An injured one limps right up to us and poses spectacularly above the lake. Although we feel competent, their flowing four-legged gait seems so much more muscular and sure than ours, their physical magnificence in keeping with the surroundings. I've not seen more than one here before and as we follow on around the ledges, we find plots

of buttercups eaten to the ground. As with other beautiful pests in
New Zealand, the chamois now seem too much of a good thing.

In typical Darrans fashion, the route takes us around on a series of
spectacular ledge systems until we arrive at the top of a really deep
chasm, narrow and dark. Watching the inevitable rocks disappear down
it, I'm struck with a vision derived from a recent movie. The Balrog – a
big rock doused in stove fuel and set alight – is dispatched into the
depths and long after the echoes die away, we're still helpless with
laughter. Everything, including humour, is simpler here.

Lazy route-finding, and a holiday atmosphere, mean that we make
it back home well after dark, again. Our bedtime reading tells us that
being overweight is in these days. We stay up late, eating.

The sun reaches the Eyrie about the right time. A pleasant laziness
envelops us; we seem to have left thoughts of further climbing behind.
We discuss various options, most of them quite appealing, and finally
settle on a slightly outlandish scheme to leave the Darrans via a hanging
valley that drops precipitously into the Tūtoko Valley. Apparently it
had been a last bastion of the almost extinct kākāpō. This is another
potential route we've looked into from above and again there are a few
question marks about the route, specifically how high and steep the
cliffs we'll be descending really are. It looks enticing, though, fitting
another piece into the local knowledge jigsaw, deepening our sense
of place We don't really want to leave the Eyrie and dawdle over the
organising. Even though we know we'll be back some time, it feels quite
nostalgic packing the gear away and it's an after-lunch departure.

As usual, the travel is quickly invigorating. We scamper quickly back
down to the Taoka, this time to traverse across the head of the glacier.
A jumbled circle of footprints in the middle of the glacier denotes
an illicit helicopter landing. Our footsteps weave a more natural line
through the slots and up to the Patuki–Underwood col.

The col is a zone of crumpled and off-colour rock at the head of
a massive faultline that stays true for several kilometres, eventually
disappearing into the Tūtoko Valley. The approach to the 'Kākāpō' lies
directly down this feature and we descend on twisted sheets of time-
warped granite, stopping frequently to marvel at the patterns within
it. The sheer face of the fault rises higher above us as we descend,
following an arrow-straight stream.

We eventually come to the end of it all: a waterfall dropping into a
world of forest and mist. We stand at the top of the cirque wall, only a
few horizontal, but many vertical, metres from easy ground. The walls
around us rise endlessly above and drop forever below, or so it seems.
Our situation is as impressive as we can imagine and it's with some
trepidation that I scramble down to the first ledges and start trying to
concoct a descent route.

It doesn't come together. Large overhangs, compact rock and the
enormous scale of everything convince us to retrace our steps. We're
tired now and the ascent back up the slabs takes on the quality of a
dream. The vertical sheets of rock above us glow deeply in the last of
the day's sunshine, wreathed in a radiant orange mist and framed in a
cobalt sky. We pitch the tent on a makeshift flat spot and then sit down,
gobsmacked, as a psychedelic sunset fades slowly to purple. A crimson
mist speeds up the wall in front – the breath of the valley dispersing
into the sky. The huge mana of this place overwhelms us. We fall asleep
in a fetid tangle in the tent.

The next day sees some early decision-making and a marked lowering in the standard of breakfast. Our options are now narrowed down to
traversing out over Underwood or reversing our route down the Donne.
Tiredness and simplicity overrule our concerns regarding the ice cliff
threat, so we wearily crampon back up to the col and down across the
Taoka. As we set the first of the abseils, we can see our descent route
unfolding below us. A series of rappels keeps us out to the side of the
fall line from the glacier and takes us neatly through the waterfall to
safety. The relaxed atmosphere of the descent contrasts markedly with

the nagging heart-in-mouth feeling of the approach day. We savour this feeling as we reverse the various bluffs and gullies, revelling less in the adventure, and more in this shared moment of satisfaction. The trip has been, not without direction, but without fixed objectives. The excitement of altering plans and moving to a different rhythm has been intoxicating, not least because we move with a common purpose.

Once in the valley, we down packs and lie on the ground. Soft cushion plants and moss support us. The smells of crushed herbs and plant juices fill our senses. The peaks are once again much higher than us and with the new perspective of having an elevated base, we idly put together future missions, already aware of our lifetimes not being long enough. Eventually we fall quiet and absorb the late summer quiet of the Darrans – distant waterfalls, the sigh of high breezes.

I love walk outs here: no tedious moraine, no tracks, no people; just steepness and the rampant Fiordland bush. We get high. The river is our main route and soon we're wet as well as filthy. Clothes rip, buttons pop, hair fills with debris. We're having a ball. The lower valley is a continuous high-speed boulder hopping session, one of my favourite things. The gloom deepens but none of us put our headlamps on, preferring the closeness of the night.

The road bridge takes us by surprise; it seems an alien structure. We sit quietly in the streambed for a while. Stepping onto the road seems like passing over some kind of threshold. We decide to capture the last moment of our trip with a photo and group together in front of the car. The flash catches us by surprise and in unison we shriek aloud, shocked, before dissolving into hysterics on the tarmac. We're not yet ready for the world; Homer seems our only refuge. We arrive back at the hut – that familiar halfway house – to find Tom and Mark there too. We stay up late recounting our various adventures, the remaining wildness within us slowly fading, delaying the need to go to sleep, reluctant to yet consider going home, to leave this place that we go.

Living the high life

We settled easily into the Eyrie; it seemed made for us and what we wanted to do, or perhaps we made it like that. Plenty of work went into it. On our annual missions in there, bad weather days invariably meant home improvements – excavations, wall building, tweaking of the custom fly-sheet set-up that Rich had made and on which our dryness depended.

There was added decoration too. Anything brought into the Eyrie had to be carried on our shoulders, yet despite this we soon sported a mirror ball and a supply of books. A troupe of glow-in-the-dark dinosaurs stood guard around the drip that was our water supply, slowly fading into the moss as time went by. Candles flickered at night, sleeping bags were kosher at any time of the day. The confines of the cave never seemed too small or stormy days any kind of imposition.

The location of the Eyrie meant that we were poised, whenever the weather eased, to get out on the local rock, of which there was plenty. It was hard, though, to go past the walls of Karetai itself. In an area renowned for the quality of its rock, Karetai, especially the East Face, stands out in terms of solidity, form and size. In having a base set high on the flanks of this, a rock climber's mountain, we had a direct line to adventure, and over a period of a decade or so, we made the most of it.

To get to the face from the Eyrie, we had unravelled a series of interlinking ledge systems. The route wasn't without excitement, however, and not to be taken lightly; enough stones roll out from under our feet, enough holds detach under our hands, and the terrain is steep enough, that we never underestimate the approach. But we worked it out, and over the years, the routes added up.

In the first lightening of the day, we're approaching the last section of ledges before we arrive at the North Ridge, from where we drop down to the Te Puoho Glacier and the East Face. Looking back, I can barely make out the Richards behind me through the thick mist. I'm at a point where the ledge ends and a rising traverse is needed to cross a rippled slab of granite above a big drop. The slab is worn smooth by a small watercourse and I suspect it has a coating of verglas, but am unable to discern it in the gloom. This is a problem of late summer trips here: the colder nights and shorter days allowing more ice to form. I stop and wait for the others.

As the light strengthens, we can see that the slab is indeed sheeted in a thin layer of ice, the frozen run-off from yesterday's rain. We're impatient to keep moving; we have a big day before us, and there's little desire to pull out a rope and belay, to break the flow for just this short section. I look more closely. The ice is very thin; between the slickness over most of the slab there are roughened high points of rock that are dry. Fingers pinching rough crystals, feet smearing on islands of dry stone, I pad slowly and precisely across the slab and it's okay. I relay to the others the need to move just so. They see it straight away and follow in the same manner; they understand. We continue, hardly breaking our stride, for this is how we move so often here, on the fine line.

At the bottom of the East Face of Karetai this first time, it's apparent that there's fabulous climbing everywhere. It all looks terrific but we haven't done our homework and can only assume where the existing routes go. On the premise that they probably follow the more obvious crack-lines, we choose the proud buttress that shoots straight up the face in front of us, drawn as usual to something that sticks out a bit. The morning sun lights the face with a friendly warmth, prompting a feeling of confidence and causing us to assess the blank steep wall, at two-thirds height, as 'not looking too bad'.

The climbing is immediately all-consuming, on rock that seems made for just such a thing. Holds are varied and interesting, cracks appear and vanish, the protection remains adequate. The stone is overwhelmingly solid, which allows us to relax, to enjoy what we're doing and we don't worry about the upcoming blank wall. We revel in the steep sun-warmed granite, the view over the remote Te Puoho catchment, above a landscape that is only like itself.

The wall, shady and more forbidding by the time we arrive there, is an affront to the air of glee that has filled us so far. As we look up, trying to fathom its secrets, we realise that we will need to apply ourselves. Richard tries first but doesn't gel with the strange and unprotectable moves off the belay. Neither do I, although I do manage to find a tiny nubbin to lower gingerly off. Not for the first time in such a situation, we look over to Rich. He sighs and racks up; he's been here before and we all know that, secretly, he loves a good hard lead sometimes.

I try to build momentum by suggesting that if Rich hangs his water bottle off the skinny loop of cord I've hung around the nubbin, it will be more secure, less likely to lift off. I don't really expect this bit of transparently over-optimistic psychology to cut the mustard but before long, probably driven more by motivations of his own, Rich is well above the water bottle and the tiny knob, and fully committed to the wall above.

It's a long and disconcerting time on the belay for Richard and me. The pitch has spaced runners that are never apparent from below; our suggestions from the belay don't seem to be that useful and we're soon advised to stop making them. The rock seems hard to read and it's a devious route that Rich takes before finally disappearing from view onto the upper wall. Apparently it's been a long and disconcerting time on the lead too, but luckily this is a situation Rich has been in before and in which he generally excels. Richard and I are pleased to manage seconding the pitch without falling, and not to have led it in the first place.

A few hours later I lead the last pitch in the dark, pulling over a steep corner onto the summit area, a chaotic jumble of rocks that serves to sort the gear, coil the ropes and generally unwind. We're on top of a little-known peak in an obscure corner of a remote part of a great big world, but home is only an hour or two from where we stand; we're living the high life.

❖

There had been icicles hanging from the lip of the cave this morning, verglas on the approach ledges again. We've left the others packing up, retreating today to the comforts of home, but Richard and I can't bring ourselves to leave; another day here is too much to pass up as another season draws to a close. We stand under the face, that great sweep of stone, again with no real idea of where we will climb. It's enough just to be here.

The line, this time, will just be pretty much straight up the middle. We know that much of the rock is climbable, however unlikely looking. We have confidence that the way will be revealed as we climb, and that the gear will come our way. Our familiarity with the face allows us a relaxation. We start at a major diagonal crack feature, breaking out onto the wall above when we feel the urge to go up. The route above follows a trajectory mostly governed by this urge – to go straight up. The long pitches flow together like an inverse flow of water, a human trickle of anti-gravity.

As we climb, the sky darkens and temperatures drop. We climb on into the cloud, the views we would normally see hidden from us. Within the cloud, though, we still know where we are and are happy to push on. Snow starts to fall, gently. High on the route, we end up at a cramped belay on a narrow ledge with the light starting to fade. Above is the last steep section. Snow is beginning to cover the holds. Richard has a couple of easy options to continue but instead carries on directly. He is quickly up the steep buttress, just shimmying up and not placing any runners until after the hard section. It's a grand gesture of ease, of connection with place.

We'll be happy descending in the dark. We know our way now
through the labyrinth of giant blocks that make up the descent route.
It will be slippery and awkward underfoot, and the terrain will look very
different, but even with the boulders covered in snow, we'll be fine.
We know our way home. We know our way home.

It's strange. I can't remember anything of our descent from Mount Milne
after climbing the South Face. Nothing of the long scramble off the peak
around to the top of the Cleft, back over the roughened rock of Tarewai,
down the long slabs and broken snowfields from Pipikari Pass, the
winding traverse around the tussock ledges back to camp. The moon
was up – I have a picture of Rich coiling the ropes on the summit, lit by
the red glow of sunset, the moon rising behind him the same colour –
but any memories I have of the descent are vague dream-like ones, of
moving through a moonlit landscape I already seemed to know well,
despite it being my first time there.

I do remember the climb itself, however – hard not to. From the
moment we'd first felt its pull, on the approach route over Tarewai,
where the face dropped away beneath our feet, and then again every
time we saw the face, we always knew we would attempt it. There was
simply no way to avoid its draw and we spent hours around camp just
looking at the face, trying to absorb some idea of what it would be like,
seeking some small nugget of familiarity to take with us when we tried
it. It would be something more than we had done before; every little bit
of confidence would help.

The first pitch was demanding, steep and thin, on glacier-worn
stone. Seconding the pitch, I snapped a hold and took a swinging fall
onto the ropes. From low on the route it was hard to parse what was
coming up and find a rhythm; the face was shady and cold. A sneaky
southerly breeze kept us flapping our arms at the belays, wearing all our
clothes and blowing on our fingers to warm them up.

Around halfway up, an exposed and beautiful pitch finished with a
layaway flake poised above a steep corner, right on the edge of the faint
buttress we were following. It was an exquisite position to be in, and as
the face started to fall away below us our excitement grew. We searched
for the line of least resistance through a landscape of difficulty,
the features subtle and discontinuous. The route was a constantly
challenging puzzle; a map of draughts. Another rope length near the top
had only a couple of runners at half-height, on a sheet of compact stone,
scalloped like a frozen wind-ruffled ocean. The situation, already wild,
became even more so the higher we climbed, aware that what we were
doing was special.

What is it now, this route? The wall is still there, the hard stone
unchanged since our ascent and much as it was before we climbed it,
our human effort only a small added dimension to something greater.
It's written up in a guidebook and there on the page is a photo, with
a line drawn on it. The line looks direct and proud, an arcane quality
with some kind of meaning, to Rich and me anyway. Perhaps it's here,
between the line on the page and the great piece of rock at the head of
Cleft Creek, that our creation fits in – the transformation of a piece of
mountainside to a human experience – a way to appreciate the qualities
of a place and touch a bigger world.

I pull myself into a crouch, push myself upwards, throw my hand to the
edge I know will be sharp and positive, and slap it hard, owning this
move as a vindication of everything that has come before it. I make
more of it than it is – a show-off celebration to myself. After latching the
arête, I lean away off my arm and lift my foot up to another hold on the
edge below my hand, rock my weight onto it and find myself standing
on the very crest of the arête – the proud edge of stone we've been
attempting and imagining for years. I'm here.

Below my feet the rock falls away. My eye follows it down to the ice tongue below the route, the rolling approach slabs above our campsite at the lake outlet, to where Turner Falls arc out to the jungles of Cleft Creek, to the lowlands of the Darrans.

Looking up, I see the sharp line of the arête carrying on for several pitches, a continuous, unbroken edge above me, a feature of unusual prominence and a rare sort of thing to climb on; something of a gift. In a moment I'll continue, probably to belay the Richards up to the small ledge above me, because it seems like a great place for some mutual congratulation. We'll spend the rest of the day climbing the arête. Along the way there'll be places where we'll teeter on its very rim, others where we'll bridge up a perfect corner on the very crest of the buttress. It will be just as we've imagined and it will be good.

The move onto the arête also marks, in some ways, a failure. To get here we've had to traverse in from the side, avoiding the difficulties of starting directly. We've tried several times to climb directly up from below but have never quite made it. From the high point of our attempts, not far above the second belay, we've been stopped by a smooth wall. A rising traverse of the wall will be needed to reach the arête from this point, but there are no visible features to follow.

We're so close, and we know, deep down, that the wall is climbable. The truth is that we're simply not brave enough. We have, all three of us, retreated carefully from just before the point of no return, unable to commit to an obviously difficult passage without the promise of further protection. There may be some further up, but there's no certainty of this and to carry on is a commitment we can't make. In another place, where we could fly in with the required gear, where we didn't feel so small in the world, we might place some bolts to remove this problem, but not here. If we can't place the gear ourselves and then take it away again to leave the rock unaltered, we don't want it; it wouldn't seem right. There are different sorts of failure.

There's always such anticipation in coming to the Central Darrans, where there are no huts, no bridges, no tracks. We exist here by fitting in, hiding from the weather under overhangs, behind our meagre stone walls and flimsy fly-sheets. We walk directly on the thin skin of the earth and carry everything on our shoulders. Within the esoteric world of climbing here, there's no guarantee of success; we walk to the bottom of a wall of rock, climb it – we hope – using what we can find and leave it as it was. I like knowing there's a place that requires you approach it on its own terms.

Here, like success, security isn't guaranteed. Here, there's an element of the unknown, an acceptance that we must fit into this world and, if nothing else, how we climb is a mark of respect for this wild place. I can only hope that those who come here in the future will be drawn to what's already here as it is now, with no 'improvements'. That they too, will be here for the unknown.

The direct start to the Hornley Arête – the blank section on the third pitch – is still the unknown. It stands there unchanged and will do even after someone else climbs it, if they forgo the temptation to use the bolts that will guarantee getting to the top. For those who finally do climb it in this style – without bolts, with the nagging fear of the unknown nipping at their heels – it will be one of the greatest climbs, in terms of the strange quality we call line, that I can think of.

An ending

All good things come to an end, apparently. The Darrans have one last surprise in store for me; one that could have happened any time before, is at the very least a ripping yarn and provides, reluctantly, a final story of sorts.

The North Face of Te Wera has been a long-standing project for me and the Richards. The face, in truth, doesn't look that appealing when viewed up close. On our first attempt, we had instead climbed a beautiful sweep of red granite on the adjacent wall of Ngaitahu Peak, because it looked more enticing. To be accurate, Te Wera looked steep and compact – in other words, difficult and hard to protect. The lower slopes also appear slick with run-off and a little grassy. Above this section a wide terrace breaks the face before it steepens up to vertical. Further up, the face steepens even further, with the top third rearing to over vertical.

Despite its size and steepness, the face isn't visible from anywhere that people tend to go. As a 'last great problem', albeit an obscure one, it has stayed in our imaginings as unfinished business, reminding us that we still want it. Still – after all this time – the same thing: the unknown.

Behind us the eastern ramparts of Madeleine, the Hollyford Valley and the Olivines are bright in the January sun. A beautiful day in a beautiful place. We – Richard, Rich and I – assess the first section as a scramble, albeit a staunch one and set off on the face. We have no idea how it will go. The scramble becomes tricky enough that we have to don our rock shoes and things become tense for a while, a couple of sections near the limits of our tolerance for soloing.

We regroup on the terrace and try to piece a line together in our minds. It's clear that we're looking for the easiest way to the top through a clearly difficult wall. The line we settle on is essentially a wish-list, a hopeful linking of the few features we can see into a continuous whole. Richard starts up the first pitch which, in the usual way, is steeper and more complicated than it looks, but at least with runners along the way, albeit devious to find.

Rich embarks on the obviously difficult-looking second pitch as Richard and I wilt on the belay in the now hot sun. He starts up a steep crack, struggles, overcomes it and disappears from sight. The rope feeds out slowly but consistently for a while before slowing to a crawl. Small tugs on the rope indicate progress being made, but painfully slowly. Eventually we hear a distant shout from Rich, which we interpret as 'watch me', the classic call of someone about to launch on a challenging and scary section. It's not something we've heard Rich say much before. On the belay, we raise our eyebrows at each other.

Time moves slowly in synch with the rope as it feeds out through the belay device. Eventually we see him come into sight, well above us and clinging to an unlikely buttress feature. Even from a distance, he's clearly working hard but it looks as if there's a lower angle section not far above; there seems to be a moment arriving. We see a distant lurch, a flurry of footwork – the moment – and then he disappears onto a hidden ledge.

Seconding the pitch is a nightmare. Above the initial steep section, which I barely manage, a long and poorly protected traverse awaits. The pack I must wear pulls me off balance and there's a moment of genuine fear as I nearly peel off, on what would have been a big swinging fall. The top bit of the pitch I can't do at all and resort to grabbing the rope, the gear, whatever gets me to the ledge. I'm strung out, mentally and physically, by the time I arrive at the belay, but then again, we all are. It is my turn to lead.

Leading turns out to be a relief. Without the weight of the pack, movement again feels natural. Above, the pitch looks manageable and the last pitch fades in my mind. I start off nervously, but there's a runner to protect the pull through the initial overhang, followed by a stance to gather my thoughts and rest. I look up. Above me there's a long sweep of rock that looks spectacularly climbable, although obviously lacking in protection. The corner where I'm resting continues up to the left as a closed and rounded seam, an awkward prospect, but further up I can see a faint opening that may allow for some runners.

I carry on, bridging and palming up the corner, following the mental arithmetic that suggests the greater likelihood of runners there. They do come but, ironically, the hardest moves on the pitch are the ones to get to them, and placing them is off-balance and challenging. The pitch is becoming hard work; I feel I'm doing what I have to rather than what I want to. I look up to the right, to the long wall. The wall beckons and now I have a runner placed I feel I can answer.

The smooth wall passes in a runnerless haze, but the climbing remains reasonable, which is the gift of perfectly solid stone. I carry on smoothly, in thrall now to the action. It happens sometimes, that you reach a point on a runout pitch when it doesn't matter anymore; when the background appreciation of seriousness is still there, but you become immersed in the climbing itself. A shout from below – the 10-metre call – brings me back to reality. Below me I see a long and barren stretch of rock. Around me I see sheer walls of smooth stone, and no alternatives to the one I'm on. Above me I can see nowhere to belay. I carry on; there is nothing else to do.

The wall provides. As the rope stretches to the end of its length, a small crack appears in the wall, an almost laser-cut slot that accepts a small cam and a tiny wire, which cluster together in the hole to form an anchor. Small but seemingly strong, and the only option. Small, and the thing I belay the others from before we abseil off, spent. Small but there, another tiny gift from the unknown.

But that's only part of the story. We spend the next few days in residence at the Eyrie, lounging around, eating and idly considering how we might approach the wall 'next time'; but we're talking about if, rather than when, we might try again. We climb another route, short but fine, on one of the nearby walls, but mostly we just relish the atmosphere.

The night before we leave it rains, and in the morning there is snow on the ground. We leave anyway, confident enough in ourselves and our descent route that we can make it down in bad weather. There's just a feeling that we should leave, and we've descended before in worse.

The weather slowly intensifies as we travel, snow turning to rain as we descend. By the time we reach the end of the abseils into the Donne, we're soaked and cold and the only thing to do is move on –

over the rain-softened snow, down the slipperiness of glacier-worn slabs, through the gathering strength of the headwaters. Everywhere, the landscape is streaked with bright lines of run-off; there's nowhere that's dry. After hours of difficult terrain, we escape the open country at the head of the valley and enter the forest. Although it's as wet as everywhere else, there's at least shelter here and we feel we can relax a little, although still with the imperative to keep moving.

We're now confined to the right bank of the river. Although the track further down is on the other side, we won't be able to cross to it. We're confident of our route, though, having done it before in similar circumstance. The escape continues, through the sodden jungle, through the dense and rotten greenery, through the continual driving rain. At times we come upon clearings and can see the valley walls of the Donne above and there's little else I've seen to match their scale and majesty in this storm. From the giant walls, rivers arc downward before morphing with the sky. It's hard to know how the valley isn't filling up, that we're not being swept away. Maybe we are.

We crouch under an overhanging boulder in the forest for a short rest. The day is taking longer than we've envisaged, but there's little to do but carry on, one dripping thicket, one rotten log, one racing torrent, one muddy bank at a time. Darkness arrives. The storm, unbelievably, is gaining in intensity. On top of the rain, now as heavy as we've ever seen it, there's thunder; the landscape around us is alive with power. We gather after another stream crossing, the last major one we think, and scoff some food, still a Moro bar to share. I slip to the back of the group, content to follow in the others' tracks for the last section, dialling back slightly on the continual drive that has possessed me, all of us, so far. We'll be back at the car in an hour or so.

The moment my life changes forever isn't much in the scheme of things – a minor event amid the wildness around us. Nothing else changes when I fall. The storm rages on. Boulders lose their grip on the bed of rivers, trees snap and grind as they fall, banks collapse. The mountains shed their skin yet again. For me, a root breaks, a hand fails to grab a saving branch. They are small things in comparison, and the moment only takes a second or two.

The fall, though, headfirst through the darkness, seems to take forever. There is time to think that this time it won't be alright, and so it turns out. There is an impact; a sickening crunch travels through my head. I lie face down in the wet ground, in the darkness. I can't move, I can't call for help. There's water around my face and I already know; there is an instant knowing. Rich is there quickly. He's seen from the corner of his eye my headlamp tumble down the bank, and he comes back to check. I hear my voice as a pathetic and distant thing. I tell him what I know – that I can't move, that I've broken my neck.

The night, from this point, is a long and arduous one for my friends. There is an order to things. Carefully, within the driving rain, they make a kind of platform of our packs and move me onto it. We do not have a tent, a fly or any kind of shelter. All we have is our climbing gear, clothes and sleeping bags; that is all. Everything firm is piled up to support me and everything soft is heaped on top – everything. It will rapidly become useless in the wet, but it will do – anything to keep away the searching cold for a time.

Tom sets off the locator beacon. Someone, somewhere, will shake their heads in disbelief. A decision is made; Richard sets off into the storm, on foot and alone, to organise the rescue.

Rich and Tom crawl in under the mound of clothes and settle in, if it can be called that, to save my life. We huddle under the heavy mass that covers us, melding with the sodden earth. I lie there for hours, Rich cradling my head on his knees. His hands seldom move and if they do they are replaced by Tom's, equally careful.

The storm reaches a climax of violence and stays there. Sheet lightning flashes in synch to deafening peals of thunder; we are in the very centre of the storm and the rain is still an unrelenting force.

I am positioned in a runnel that has now become a streamway. Rich and Tom crouch around me, the water rising up their legs, the cold racking their bodies. Together, we wait.

❖

For me, within those first few hours, something else is happening. Under the heap of sodden clothes, in the driving rain, held close by my stoic companions, there is a decision still to be made and it is mine alone. I knew, as soon as it happened, what my injury was and I knew also what it meant – that this would be the end, perhaps not of everything, but of most of it, that the bulk and heft of my life would be forever different, never again like this one.

I lie there in the storm, aware of the situation but comfortable nonetheless. The elemental world around me is playing my grand finale, or so I like to think, even now imagining a connection between us that is so finally, so obviously, only mine to perceive. It is a vanity, no doubt, that I feel these mountains cry and rage for me; but already I cry and rage for myself and as I lie there under the raucous peals of thunder, within the gothic drama of the storm, I wonder what I should do. There is a decision still to be made.

To start with, it seems that it might be easy, that I might just drift away. I feel for a time that this is indeed happening, as my breath gets slowly smaller and more distant from me. Time passes in reverie, in reminiscence. I am content to float for a while, an hour or two perhaps, but after a time this feeling passes, and I know that if I am going to die here, it will need to be a conscious decision and it is still to be made.

There is a horror in contemplating a life of immobility, perhaps greater if you have lived a particularly physical life, one in which that physicality has given purpose to your existence, but perhaps not; I'm sure most people would understand. But to now do this thing, to decide not to live, I need to involve someone else. I need to talk to Rich, to ask him to just hold my mouth and nose closed for long enough; that would

do. We are close and he may be thinking the same thoughts. I imagine
he would do this thing for me.

I don't ask, although I come close. I don't ask because there is, away
deep down, some tiny kernel of hope, a latent lust for life, that stops me.
I don't ask, not because I don't want to put Rich on the spot, but because
I want to stay in the world a while longer. To survive because there
might be something more. There is, I know, a massive effort being put
into saving my life and somehow the decision is made for me. All I can
do, lying there in the storm, in the hands of others, is to follow the small
thread of instinctual, primal hope that may mean survival. I wait there
unmoving, and hope that survival will be worth it.

— **PART FIVE** —

MAGMA

Magma forms from the partial melting of the earth's mantle – the greywacke, schist and granite that make up the crust, reimagined yet again. It swirls, molten and unstructured, beneath the surface of the earth and can take many forms upon emerging. It's forced into the world, usually, through a cataclysmic event, a fracturing of existing structure, and although its basic make-up is already in place, its future shape depends on the forces applied to it and how it responds to change.

Sometimes it will become a glowing river of lava, or go on to contain crystals that sparkle with brilliance, or become the foundation of a fertile soil in which to grow living things. It can, too, end up being fractured and broken, a stone that is irrevocably weakened. It is possible, that magma may never make it to the surface at all, and be lost to the world. More than anything, magma is about potential.

Rescue

Richard makes swift time out to the road, the car, the telephone at
Milford. He is able to explain to the rescue team why the beacon has
been set off, and what needs to happen. A ground crew is dispatched
from Te Anau. Guided by Richard through the torrential rain and
difficult terrain of the lower Donne, they arrive around 4 a.m., just
in time to stave off the hypothermia dogging the three of us under
our sodden heap of nylon. Warm drinks are conjured, dry clothes and
sleeping bags produced. My neck is immobilised, allowing Rich to
finally move again. I'm placed under a low fly and wrapped in further
warm things.

I am unable to remain detached from my predicament and from the
stretcher I lie in, the SAR side of me does its best to coordinate what's
happening. I drift in and out of consciousness, issuing instructions
that may or may not be only in my head. One thing that does become
apparent, just before pick-up, is that the stretcher I'm in is inappropriate
for flying. No one had noticed and some consternation and rejigging are
required to put it right.

A helicopter leaves before first light from Te Anau, crewed by rescue
legends Richard 'Hannibal' Hayes and Lloyd Ferguson. The storm, still
raging and centred directly over us in the Darrans, necessitates on-
the-edge flying around its fringes, and I can't be lifted out before 9
a.m. Moments before we're wrenched out on the longline through the
dripping bush, the stretcher attendant, Stu, swears at the malevolence
of the world that means he has to do this; 'I hate this shit' are the last
words I hear before lifting off. Spinning under the helicopter through
the sodden Fiordland sky, having tried desperately to stay awake and
control my fate, I start to drift off. There is little now I can do for myself.

After the pick-up, things are still pretty touch and go. The helicopter
is forced to fly back around the storm, a slight lifting of the cloud over
a Fiordland pass allowing us to meet the medically equipped rescue
helicopter in Te Anau, where the process of rewarming my severely
hypothermic body can begin. My core temperature hovers around 31° C
for many hours, somewhere near the cut-off temperature for survival. I
make it, but only just.

Meanwhile, Rich, Tom and the entire rescue team are winched out,
one by one, under another helicopter, as coldness and the reality of
reversing the terrain is assessed. The busy Milford road is closed down
for the operation and many people are involved; the rescue is a big deal.
The wave of effort to ensure my survival has rolled into action. It began
with pushing the button on the beacon and Richard running off into the
night. It continues to this day.

Realisation

Once I'm in hospital in Dunedin, my head is tractioned and my spine
realigned but the damage is done; the outcome will eventually be
recorded as a C4, incomplete tetraplegia. A small realignment of my
neck vertebrae into the delicate tissues of my spinal cord – a deviation
of only a few millimetres – is enough to change my life forever. I have
hazy memories of a metal ring, a 'halo', being screwed into my head and
then attached to the bedhead, of my body being stretched in some kind
of medieval torture technique.

Once thermally stabilised, I'm transferred to Christchurch Hospital
to begin a three-week stint in the intensive care unit, where persistent
lung infections have another go at killing me. My early memories are
of fevered dreams, of a slow-growing awareness of my condition, of
people murmuring in my ear, telling me it will be alright. For many
days, the reality of my situation eludes me. I know that something isn't
right but it takes a long succession of dreams, interspersed with brief

forays into reality, that together bring me to the realisation of what has happened, and what it means.

❖

To start with I find myself back at Homer, the hut where I've spent so much time over the years, sitting on the couch next to the potbelly stove, warming up by the fire. I feel comfortable and at home, but have the feeling that something is wrong. I can't say what it is. People are moving around but no one talks to me, seemingly busy with other things. There's an argument going on outside and something urgent seems to possess the occupants of the hut. There's some kind of anomaly, a growing sense of unease.

I try to rise from the couch but can't. I ask someone passing me by why this is so, but they don't say, avoiding my eyes. I'm desperately thirsty but no one brings me a drink, even when I ask. I fight down a rising sense of panic as I try to rise from the couch, but fail again. A sense of helplessness comes over me. I hear rain on the roof, which always means the same thing here: wait until it clears up. So, with nothing else to do and no way of doing it anyway, I sit back and wait.

The waiting continues, but the location changes. I find myself sitting cross-legged by a roadside intersection. A fine sand has drifted and settled around me and it seems that I am a wayside marker, a mute warning of sorts to any passers-by. Other debris protrudes from the sand around me and it's apparent that the road is one long travelled. A low gloom hangs over the forsaken crossroads and there's an air of antiquity.

I am mostly alone and time passes very slowly. An occasional traveller arrives. They are all old and thin. They carry on and they have little to say as they pass. An air of sadness hangs over them, as though sorrow is a constant in this place. I sit unmoving among the drifting sand, and continue to wait.

My inner world becomes increasingly mysterious; strange physical settings that themselves become puzzles to be solved, riddles to be explored, nebulous quests to be embarked upon. These problems are incredibly complex, on the very edge of what I can know. It seems desperately important to work them out and I'm consumed by an urgency to do so, but whenever I feel I'm approaching some kind of reckoning, the world changes and there's never an explanation.

The worlds I find myself in are multi-dimensional, convoluted and maze-like, full of physically tight places and cobwebs and darkness. There are meetings with people I know, but these are out of context and there's an air of strangeness about them. I hunt for answers, but one problem often becomes several and just as I feel I have solved something, it appears I have not. A constant low level panic stays with me throughout and although the dream worlds keep me occupied, I suspect there's something beyond what I know.

For what feels like many days, I'm trapped within something I can only describe as a 3-D newspaper, a puzzle of contemporary events that I need to work my way through. I finally feel I'm reaching a conclusion, that the intense concentration and hard work have paid off, that I've gained some deeper understanding. I see a brightening of the sky above me that hasn't been there before. With growing exultation, I move towards the light, bursting with a new hope. Perhaps now I'll understand, or at least, I won't need to anymore.

I emerge into yet another world. There's a person there. She seems familiar and she tells me, not for the first time and in words I've heard before, that I'm wrong; that this new world, just like the last and the one before that, has no salvation. Not for me. I can't bear it so I leave. Somewhere, surely, there's a better place. I'll keep looking, so I close my eyes.

This becomes the pattern of my days: long indeterminate periods spent mostly in the strange new netherworld of the drugged-up ICU patient.

It's better than the alternative, however, because interspersed with the dreams are excursions into reality – though it takes a while for me to recognise these for what they are, to grasp that reality is what happens when my drug regime is sufficiently reduced for me to relate to the actual world.

The first of these occasions has its humorous side. 'Si' and 'Phil' are the surgeons who cheerfully explain the intricacies of my upcoming spinal fixation surgery.

'Firstly, let us introduce ourselves – I'm Si.'

'And I'm Phil.'

I recall a Si and Phil as radio talkback hosts so this seems too odd to be true, but I let them continue, bemused by the change of scene.

'We're going to explain the procedure to you so you don't have to worry about it. And, just to let you know, we're total experts in our field. Aren't we, Phil?' says Si.

'Yes, exactly, Si, we really know what we're doing. Years of experience.'

They laugh in unison, and then explain their intention to fuse the vertebrae in my neck to stabilise the injury site.

'Now, we intend to go in from the front,' says Phil. 'We just prefer it that way. Eh, Si?', and Si agrees, in on some secret joke.

'However there can be problems doing it like that, so we just thought we'd run through them with you first.'

I wonder why, but keep that thought to myself as Phil is still talking. '… to go in from the front requires that we have to get past, um, what is that thing, Si?'

'The windpipe.'

'Yeah yeah, that too, but I mainly meant…'

'Oh yes, I know – the carotid artery – that's it, eh Si?'

Si agrees and they both laugh again, pleased with the slickness of their routine. Somehow, they seem very funny and when it becomes apparent that we're about to go into surgery, I'm quite comfortable with the idea of Si and Phil – crack international surgeons – excavating into my spine. In fact I'm all for it. I give my consent, which appears to be the object of the discussion, and forget what happens next.

❖

An intensive care unit, for the patients in it, is a strange blend of dreams and reality at the best of times. At worst, it's both a waking and unconscious nightmare. It is seldom boring.

Over a couple of weeks of real time, an ICU dream theme becomes more prevalent in my mind, and I slowly become more used to it, and even find it somewhat comforting. I wake one day, though, in an unfamiliar ward, the beds arranged differently and the outside light coming from a different angle. At the foot of the bed stands Tariq, which is odd, as he was my nurse in the other, familiar, ICU ward.

'You were in an explosion, Dave,' he says. 'At the bank. In Berlin. You're now in a German ICU. Don't you remember?' This explains a lot – why the ward seems different, more orderly somehow – but it doesn't explain his presence.

'I'm just here for you, Dave, wherever you may be,' he adds, which should feel reassuring but instead makes me suspect that something is being withheld. It turns out that the different ward layout is the result of a move to another bed. Some nurses are known for their offbeat humour; I still don't know if Tariq made up the bank explosion story, or I did.

The ICU is a hotbed of other activity too. Across from my bed a door leads into a small office. From there a narrow stairway rises into the ceiling, but I can only surmise what happens up there and no one will tell me. People come and go; there's a furtiveness to their activities. When I move beds, I get another angle on it. I can now hear what they get up to in the ceiling: it's a music radio station. I hear only pieces at first, faint snatches of ethereal chanting, screaming industrial punk, a banshee wailing the like of which I've never heard again, interspersed with beautiful melodies and soothing ethnic drum beats. It seems they're a pretty alternative bunch up there in the ceiling.

There's some construction stuff going on up there too. Through a gap in the ceiling above my bed I see glimpses of their activities: screaming industrial grinders that somehow make no noise, the bright lights of superhot fires. At one point I see one of them – a crazed mad scientist type with welding goggles and wild hair. Looking down, he sees me too and laughs maniacally before bending back to his task; to his gas torch and glass tubes.

I complain regularly about the work in the ceiling, to the extent that one day I lose my rag entirely and rage at the nurse. 'This is an *intensive care unit!*' I scream. 'How the fuck can it operate like this, with all the noise and construction dust over everything?'

One of the nurses agrees, ostentatiously dusting my bed off until I'm satisfied. That night, the obese woman in the paddling pool next to me dissolves in her own bodily fluids. I don't see it, I just know it happened, and when I mention it to one of the nurses next morning she looks at me, as if to ask how I know. I look meaningfully back; I don't know how, I just do.

There is another intervention, in which I'm brought out of the drug world to give my consent for a tracheostomy. Debate is raging over the decision and someone has decided that I'll be capable of making up my own mind on the matter. A kind of Si and Phil debate carries on around me but this one is much less fun. I make a decision – 'whatever' – and sink back into la-la-land.

Something changes for me after this glimpse of reality. Whenever I start to become aware of real life, I quickly take myself elsewhere, knowing perhaps that the day will come when this won't be possible. For the time being though, there's an endless changing landscape to be found in the light panels above my bed – Scandinavian winter scenes or oceanic vistas usually – and always somewhere to be transported to. These worlds are always beautiful and I stay within them as much as I can; the lights keep me protected for now.

I've always related to fish. I've spent much of my life as an angler and studied them closely, so it doesn't surprise me to discover that I've somehow become one; that I'm now a squirming, elongated fish creature struggling in a net. And not just any kind of net. This one is long and tubular, like the bags that oranges come in sometimes – a kind of stretchy tube that widens as I wriggle though it and closes again as I pass. It's hard work, all the wriggling. It seems to be taking a long time to get anywhere, but I feel that there's a purpose to my struggles, so I persist.

The water I'm swimming in becomes shallower and soon I'm just below the surface. I glimpse a person above me and through the distortion of the surface, I can see they're wearing a white lab coat. I ask whether I'm some kind of scientific experiment. A nice man, tall and Indian, replies in the affirmative and it somehow makes sense. I'm trying something out – something important – and I need to keep on trying. I might learn something.

I continue swimming out of the water and into the sunlight. As I emerge into the air, it's bright and new and I wriggle and splash, a newly landed fish in the shallows. Still around me, though, is the tight net I'd expected to be freed from as I left the water. I continue to thrash, arms pinned to my side, trying to shuck it off, but it remains and I realise that the experiment isn't over; I've emerged from the water without drowning and yet the net is still constricting my movements. As it turns out, the experiment is only just beginning.

This final foray from dreams into reality moves me closer to my first proper realisation of what has occurred and what it means. Each time I wake, there's less and less to differentiate one world from the other. Everything outside of the dreams is another version of the claustrophobia within them; the lack of movement, the mask over my face. I'm reluctant to face up to it.

Breathing becomes another version of the claustrophobic dread of being unable to move. Whenever the fluid filling my lungs builds to the point I feel I'm drowning, pus is sucked from them with a machine that sounds something like a vacuum cleaner. It probably isn't pus, but it sure feels like it. My lungs are also beaten and percussed to dislodge the rattling fluids within them.

My voice is reedy and thin and communication by voice becomes impossible anyway, with the insertion of a tracheal breathing tube. I'm confined to blinking in reaction to alphabet letters to spell out the words I want to convey, a frustrating process for everybody. At one stage we hire a lip reader for some important conversation. I start to understand vulnerability, a feeling that will dog me for a long time to come.

Life in the intensive care ward is generally grim. People die around you, there is an air of seriousness and you know in your bones that it's a place to move on from as soon as possible. I need to get out, into the fresh air, but the first time doesn't go so well.

Three weeks or so into ICU, my friends take me outside – the bed is wheeled into the lift, down a few levels into the basement, and then through the doors of the ambulance bay to the outside world. The air is dry and windy. Above me I can hear some tree branches moving in the wind. Despite not being able to raise my head, I can tell there's a nor'wester brewing.

I'd been warned – they've seen a lot, these nurses – that I may find it difficult, perhaps a bit overwhelming. They're right, but it isn't a delayed reaction to my accident or the first breath of fresh air after the stifling intensity of the ICU ward that makes me cry. It isn't that, and it isn't the drugs or the memory of what I've been through; it's just the realisation that this life I'd led until now is finished, that the world in which I'd spent my life, is no longer mine. Funny, that my first venture outdoors becomes a marker of the ending of my outdoor life.

Recovery

Despite this sobering glimpse of reality, it has to be faced up to, and my motivation to be gone from the ICU becomes obsessive. I can only leave, however, if I can breathe unaided. The last week of being weaned off the ventilator, and learning to draw life from the air without it, is among the hardest times I remember. I start with increments of a few minutes off the ventilator, slowly building up to half an hour, an hour, then slowly more, even achieving periods of sleep. Every inhalation is an effort and every other moment is an exercise in maintaining calm. It takes a week of effort, but at the end of it I'm able to breathe without assistance. I'm ready – desperate, in fact – to move on.

I move to the spinal unit in Burwood, the view out the ambulance window on the way reminding me that there's still a world beyond hospital. Returning to it seems a distant prospect. The spinal ward, though, is something of a relief after the confines of the ICU. Although it's part of the hospital, there's an air of a long-stay lodge about the ward. The rooms open onto gardens and plenty of light and sun make it into the rooms. I settle in for the long haul.

It's not easy. The first few weeks bring a growing clear-headed realisation of my condition. It's hard to ignore how physically broken I am; that I can't do much more than shrug one of my shoulders, the left one. The internal horror of immobility is with me most of the time. I'm a helpless bundle of floppy limbs and everything must be done for me; cleaning, feeding, toileting and the simplest of movements require someone else to perform them. There's a total loss of independence; dignity is an impossibility.

The dreams follow me to Burwood, dogging my sleep, and I find little respite from the low-grade terror that visits me at night, but from the beginning my friends are there. When I wake terrified and paralysed at night they're there by my bedside, and they stay there, calming me until the fear subsides. They even organise their own roster. Through the nights they sit by my bed reading books, playing games and doing crosswords, staying until the horrors subside. After a couple of weeks of this, I remember waking from my first night without dreaming, awash with relief that an untroubled mind might just be achievable.

This is the one constant I have left – my people: my friends and family. For the next few months, as I tremble and shake my way through my physio exercises, they egg me on, rejoicing in the minor triumphs, supporting me through the more frequent hard times. They make real food for me; I'm in hospital for many weeks before I have to eat a hospital meal. They stage potluck dinners in the dining hall, they whizz up healthy smoothies, they stretch and massage my withering limbs. Later, as I improve, they will carry me off to parties and take me to movies. In increments, I will gradually realise that there will be life after this, that it will be worth it, because of them. My mother and sister alternate their visits from Australia, and are there pretty much the whole time. I reconnect with them, and better than I have for ages; it's a small but important blessing.

Other interludes keep me in touch with the outside world. My bed is wheeled outside one afternoon to spend some time under a courtyard tree. Friends arrive from Wānaka and they have a surprise for me; Molly seems confused until her paws are lifted onto the bed and she catches my smell. She bounds up onto the bed, all wriggles and whining, gives me a once-over licking and settles down with me for the next hour, tangled in my catheter tube but happily reunited. I lie there with tears streaming down my face; all is not lost. My dog still loves me and I obviously still smell the same.

❖

My body transforms, in a dispiritedly rapid way, from the vehicle that
carried my life around, to something of a letdown. I lose 15 kilos from
an already lean frame. From being the source of much of my joys, my
body becomes a source of infinite frustration, verging on disgust. On a
good day, there's a science-project fascination in observing my physical
decay, but mostly it's a hard thing to watch – a sort of slow-motion
horror as my body morphs into something other. My muscles waste
quickly, my joints appear swollen and distorted. My skin becomes dry
and scaly, my feet purple and blotchy. I develop a curvy hunch back
torso, a 'tetra belly' and my body is plagued with random twitches. Any
physical effort is negated by bouts of reactionary spasm, the result
of a newly randomised nervous system. The roadblock in my upper
spine means that my physical reactions are now unmoderated by any
conscious control; the reflexes that have saved me many times in the
past are now an uncontrollable function that causes endless frustration
and discomfort.

There's a definite order to my recovery programme. After the first
few weeks of lying horizontally, any rise from a sitting position brings
on a change of blood pressure that floods me with nausea. The first
time the overhead hoist lifts me out of bed, everyone cheers, an instant
before I faint in front of them. Once I reach a certain equilibrium,
I'm able to start with my physiotherapy programme, but it's a
tentative start.

Over the first month or so, the tilt table becomes my nemesis.
The table is a narrow, padded plinth onto which I'm strapped in a
horizontal position, like a withered Frankenstein's monster. The table
is then slowly raised at one end until nausea sets in. To start with,
the queasiness happens at a dispiriting 30 degrees, before I need to
be lowered flat. Each session requires several rounds of raising and
lowering, a repetitive cycle of near fainting and nausea. It's something I
yearn to move on from, but there's nothing else in the physio gym that I
can physically do. I need to get moving, though, so am forced to endure
the tilt table until my body can withstand a restored gravity.

Once I've adapted to being upright again, there's a progression through the gym's various devices. I'm hooked up to electrode pads and introduced to an electrical stimulation bike to get my legs moving again; my muscles clench and work, without any input from me, eventually leading to some improvement. A range of unusual exercises restore whatever coordination and strength I can muster. My arms haul on pulley systems attached to tiny weights; I remember bench pressing a foam dumbbell until exhaustion and ending up being pinned under it. I progress to a standing frame that supports my weight, fall off it more than once, and then graduate to a walking frame, a tenuous but exciting step forward.

Gradually, the more practical aspects of my future life are rehearsed. Transferring to and from wheelchairs, beds and eventually cars is practised relentlessly. The gym is a source of physical inspiration to most of us on the ward; we all try harder because we see people who do improve. Some leave on their feet and even if they don't, we all still harbour the hope that we will too, and physical effort is the only real way to create the chance of achieving it. Most of us try really hard, but not all. In some, I see the light go out.

I remain in the ward for seven long months and my initial fragility slowly becomes some sort of robustness. I might not be able to do much physically but I set off on the road of adaptability, of learning this new way to live, and hope for the best.

The spinal ward is very different from the world of my previous experience. The people around me are damaged and struggling, both physically and mentally. I alternate between being an observer of damaged souls and being passionately involved with 'getting better' myself. All of us on the ward struggle, and I'm constantly impressed with my fellow inmates, each adjusting to a major life change in their own ways. Around me there is plenty of sorrow, depression and anger, but what I mostly see is flinty resolve and determined positivity.

Much emphasis is put on physical recovery, a practical thing for life after the ward, but the mental and emotional recovery is the hardest to get on top of. There are many emotional downs – wild mood swings, bouts of anger and depression and overwhelming sadness – but there are small triumphs too, and they're often related to physical milestones: the first toe wriggle, the first wobbly stand, a first tiny hard-on.

To start with, I hang my hat on my physical improvement. I can't imagine any kind of decent existence unless I get 'better' and after the first few months there's been too little of that to give me much hope. Although I keep trying, I slowly sink deeper into a sort of low-grade misery, a fatigue brought on by the potential never-endingness of it all. It becomes hard to see the point of making the effort. The mental and emotional advances are harder to put my finger on than the physical, but I realise, after a while, that I'm at least surviving.

The medical team never gives me a prognosis for the posssible extent of my physical recovery, although there's some mention of timeframes. A standard utterance, while on the ward, is that it's still 'early days'. I'm told that a window of approximately two years is when most recovery is likely to take place, but also that everyone is different. Nothing is set in stone and nothing too much is held up in the way of hope. It doesn't make for complicated maths, though, to plot the current rate of improvement over two years and come up with an approximation of where you might end up.

I suspect everyone in this situation reaches the point where certain futures become obvious, the point where you realise that, unless something changes, there are three clear potential outcomes: putting up forever with the persistent sadness, making some kind of effort to not be miserable, or removing that sadness by killing yourself.

I can imagine it wouldn't need much to push you towards death when life seems endlessly unappealing, but it's not that easy. For the severely disabled, it's a difficult thing to organise. Without the physical capacity to do it themselves, they require help from someone else – a huge test of love or friendship. Although I looked into it, I never asked. To my mind, death means the end of pretty much everything, so it doesn't take a great deal to make life seem more appealing. Just the odd little thing, the occasional reminder that, if this one thing seems worth it, other things may too.

Once you've made this decision, continuing with life means there are two choices – to stay miserable or to make some kind of effort not to be. In this new life, that people were there for me – that I was surrounded by love – was apparent, but a life needs some personal satisfaction, something uniquely its own, to seem worthwhile. It needed something of my own making, and for a long time I could see nothing.

There was no one big moment, no blinding flash of insight, more a series of small events that kept me going. I figured that if I stuck with it, and went on looking, one day a door might open. I would settle in for the long haul and in the meantime I would take whatever interesting things came my way. It turned out that many of these involved a degree of humour. Cripple life throws up surreal situations unavailable to most people. Wheelchair crashes, gymnasium mishaps, the general pathetic quality that accompanies spinal injury – it takes time to appreciate their latent humour.

One day I'm sitting by the open door of our room in my power wheelchair, reading a book. Nick's in his bed, also reading. There's a strong nor'wester outside and a gust blows the curtain onto me, resting momentarily on the control toggle of my chair, which I've forgotten to turn off. Instantly the chair drives forward into the doorfame, hard. The wind eases for a moment, the weight of the curtain eases and the chair backs up – which then pulls the curtain tight and pushes the toggle down again. I crash hard into the wall again, and then again, and again, physically unable to brush off the heavy curtain to stop it. This goes on for a while. Nick asks if he should call for help, and I'm about to say yes, when from nowhere, I start laughing at the absurdity of it. Nick starts up too and, as I carry on being repeatedly bashed into the wall, we find ourselves caught up in a bout of hysterical laughter. Eventually the curtain falls off the controller and the situation sorts itself out as we slowly calm down. Although it's easy to scream in frustration at events like this, it also helps to realise that there is a certain novelty to being a helpless cripple, and it may be better to embrace it if you can.

One day another unexpected adventure comes along, and with it a re-engagement of sorts with the natural world. The Travis wetland area, close to the spinal ward, has a wheelchair-friendly walkway around the perimeter. It becomes handy as a place to go and relax with my friends, watch the ducks and socialise. When Richard arrives for a visit one sunny day we decide to circumnavigate the wetland, something I haven't done yet.

But halfway around, we're caught out when a southerly front roars in. The temperature drops radically as blasts of horizontal rain buffet us and we pick up our speed to try and get back before I'm overwhelmed by the cold. Richard layers me up and, ponchos flapping and hands beginning to freeze, we head for home. I lose feeling and function in my hands, and as we cross the road to the hospital I'm unable to control the chair properly and Richard has to flag the traffic to a halt. Back in my room I have a nasty spasm attack and shiver violently for half an hour, but I've found the wildness of the storm invigorating. It's a reminder that, with some fine tuning and better clothing, I may be able to experience the elements somehow. Some of the other excitements visited on me, though, are less uplifting.

The ward is deathly quiet, half an hour after the midnight 'turning round'. Those of us unable to roll over in bed are turned by a team every three hours, throughout the night, in order to prevent pressure sores. I'm now positioned on my right side, legs curled and up and aching to get to sleep. I've had a bad night so far. To varying degrees, spinal patients suffer from muscle spasm. For me it comes and goes, ranging from an occasional twitching in my legs, through to full-body convulsions. Medication is necessary, but not always enough. Tonight, my spasm is worse than normal.

Other things are adding to my general bad mood. Nick, my permanent room-mate, is sound asleep – all good there, but no one to talk to. Pete, an older guy in the bed opposite, has fallen asleep, as he always does, with his TV on. I know he's sleeping because he snores, loudly. Normally, I would page the nurse to come and turn the TV off. In fact I already have, but he woke during the process and insisted that he was still watching. The nurse relents but ten minutes later he's asleep again, the TV still on, the snoring ramped up a notch. I slip my headphones on and eventually drift off, listening to music, twitching under the blanket, grumpy that I have to put up with this shit.

I wake when I'm turned again, exchange the usual drowsy pleasantries with the two eccentrics that comprise the team, scoff some anti-spasmodic meds and try to go back to sleep, but forget to ask them to turn off Pete's TV. I try for a while longer to ignore the noise and the spasm, now increasing, but it's useless. Nick, curiously, is still fast asleep, deep in a cocktail of drugs. Lucky him, he's usually the one in this situation. I can't sleep. I need some pills. I'll have to buzz the nurse.

The call buzzer, a big red button on a small white plastic box, is my only means of asking for help. The button has to be pushed to activate the buzzer, which is wired through to a red light above the hallway door to the room. When you push the button, a buzzer sounds in the hall and the light turns on. Three pushes means you need urgent help, one is a more general request.

Using the call buzzer, however, depends on quite a few things being lined up. First, I have limited ways of pushing it and the system we've settled on isn't foolproof. The box is taped, with surgical tape, onto the pillow next to my head. To activate the buzzer, I have to flick my head sideways and hit it with enough force to depress the button. It often takes a few goes and it's a bit hard on my neck. Whenever I'm turned, the buzzer is re-taped onto the other side of my pillow, in this case, on the left. The position of the buzzer is key.

Tonight, those things aren't lined up. For starters, Alan has reused the sticky tape, so that the box is dangling further away from me than is ideal. Second, during the repositioning, the box has moved further from my head than normal. Third, my spasm has caused my head to also move so that the box is now – just – out of reach. I don't notice any of this until the nurses have gone back to their station at the other end of the hall.

For half an hour or so, I try repeatedly and ever more desperately to activate the buzzer until I just have to lie there, frustrated and helpless. Feeling wound up and thrashing around isn't good for my spasm; my body clenches tight, curling me into a ball that jerks me closer to the edge of the bed. Another spasm racks me, my blanket falls off the side of the bed and my head slips off the end of my pillow. Reaching the buzzer is now completely beyond me and I need help more than ever. I feel the edge of the mattress slowly giving way under me, moving me ever closer to the floor, to all sorts of unpleasantness. It's only a matter of time before I fall.

I yell out, or try to, but my feeble lungs can manage no more than a kind of whining squeak, nowhere near enough to be heard over the background noise of Pete's TV. Normally, during the day, there would be traffic along the hallway. Now, in the middle of the night, there's no one and there won't be until the next turning, some two hours away. Soon, I'll be on the floor, probably injured, tangled in my catheter tubes, writhing in spasm and no one will know. Each time I jerk – every 20 seconds or so now – I slip closer to the edge.

I try screaming but the sound that comes out is more like a pathetic squeal. Even so, there's no better option, so I keep it up. I sound ludicrous; I'm just hoping that I make a big enough crash on impact to alert somebody to the problem. My head hangs well over the edge and I stare down at the floor; it seems far way. Streaky hospital lino here I come; I'm on my way.

'Eh, what?' says Pete. Half asleep, he reaches up and turns off the TV, out of reflex. He has woken, enough maybe. With all my might I manage a high-pitched stage whisper as I slide out of the bed – 'Help me, Pete, push the buzzer.' He wakes enough to comprehend something and pushes his buzzer – once only, but that should do in the middle of the night; someone will now come. He is asleep again before the nurses arrive.

I'm rescued in the nick of time. I voice my displeasure at everything. Apologies are made but eventually, as it does, humorous banter takes place. Later, I will lay an official suggestion about TV use, but I can't get down on Pete too much; he did wake up after all. Nick slept through the whole thing, I have to recount the story the next day.

In the end, I realise that I need to plan ahead and make sure these things don't occur; that my life is different now. Helplessness, reliance on others, planning for weakness: these are the new things I need to incorporate into my life.

Eventually, seven months after entering the spinal ward, I'm deemed ready for integration back into society. My last week in Burwood sees me stagger a few metres on the walking frame, cheered on by a supportive crowd of physiotherapists, fellow cripples, friends and family. I start to feel some hope that there may be a future in which I walk again. Mostly, though, I need to progress in other ways. I leave the ward for an unknown life back home, an uncertain future. I try to insert the concept in my head of starting off on a big new adventure but there's a lack of excitement, a lack of heart, a feeling that life will now be a series of chores, of making up the days, of something altogether pathetic.

I do, though, feel an obligation. At my leaving hospital party at my friend Brigette's I'm compelled to make a small speech to convey my gratitude to all the people who have helped me. So much effort has gone into my recovery – so much love – that all I can think of to express, apart from a heartfelt thanks, is a public resolve to make a go of it; to promise that I won't give in, that I'll give it my best shot. It seems as good a motivation as any. In my heart, however, I have my doubts.

Reality

I'd been warned about how hard it would be returning home. Even though getting out of the spinal ward is something that has to happen and something I crave, after several months there's a sort of comfort in being in hospital. The big wide world is a scary place. The reality is made even harder by having to move into an unfamiliar house: mine, with its narrow doorways and stairs, is unsuitable. This, as it turns out, is the least of my problems.

The entirety of my new life is unrecognisable, a pale imitation of what it was. My place in the world has gone, nothing is the same. Everything around me is a reminder of this and I begin my re-entry by doing all that seems left to me: crying, a lot.

Apart from no longer having a job to go to, a basic structure is missing from my everyday life. Checking the weather had always been the first activity of the day and I continue with this routine for some time until I realise that I no longer need to know; there's no work to go to, no chance of getting caught out in a storm. The other rhythms of life that relate to the natural world also fade from my life. The phases of the moon, the tides on the coast, the snow conditions up high, all slowly disappear from the background knowledge I carry with me. Any given day's activities are now shaped around the basic chores of washing, dressing and eating, and the motivations of my life revolve around whatever's going on in my head. At least I have my mind, although danger lurks there too. I think a lot, maybe too much. It seems, for a while, that it's all I have left to do.

Many physical matters I've never considered arise as new problems to be solved. Bowel and bladder care, circulation, temperature regulation, muscle spasms become the new vocabulary of my body. I learn the situations and activities that cause me to tense into spasm, the drugs to use, the drugs to avoid, how to recognise hot from cold. I learn new and arcane skills. I've now perfected the art of sleeping in one position, unmoving. I can lie on my back all night without turning over, not by choice but by necessity. It's harder than it sounds, but I now sleep heavy and unmoving, like a corpse. That snores.

Movement is one of the pillars on which our lives are built. I squirm in my chair, hardwired to move. There's never a moment when I don't have the urge to jump up and do something: a bike ride, splitting a batch of firewood, weeding the garden, reaching for something on a high shelf. Every morning, as my chair is wheeled up to my bed, I regard it with disgust, but there's no other real choice, since I'm also sick of my bed. All I can do is embrace whatever physicality is possible. As a way of staying in touch with my body, I embark on an esoteric and entertaining yoga journey with my good friend Keri. I crawl and hang, struggle and bend my way through our sessions. Initially there's a sense of desperation in me, a drive to improve, and for a while I do. Gradually, though, my yoga becomes more of a physical maintenance exercise and a place to regain my mental poise. Although my body feels functionally useless, there's a comfort in using it in familiar ways, even if it's someone else doing much of the moving.

For quite a while after coming home I remain focused on getting back walking, and for a while I do make progress. I can be helped into a standing position in my walking frame and on a couple of occasions I manage to wobble the length of my driveway, some 15 metres or so. Despite my best efforts, though, it never becomes a consistent thing. Early on there's an assessment for my lump-sum ACC payout. I go into the interview knowing that should I be assessed as 80% or more disabled (by an arcane process of applying points to various body parts and subtracting what I've got left that functions), I will qualify for the full payout. I'm so focused on proving to myself that I'm getting better, that I talk up my achievements and come out having scored 76 per cent, and with about $20,000 less than I probably should have. As I leave, the assessor says, 'Most people talk up their problems, Dave.'

It takes a while – well, past the early days, at least – for me to accept that walking, in particular, isn't going to improve. It's not just my legs. A particular source of frustration is not being able to use my hands well. Although my left hand recovers to the point of being able to hold a pen and write, slowly, the applied uses for them both are minor. Former activities that seem appropriate – fly-tying and jewellery-making, anything demanding finer motor skills – become unattainable.

Having lived a hands-on life, it becomes a major frustration to be useless at any practical level. All around me, all the time, are things to be done that I can't do: household chores, minor fix-it jobs, the day-to-day tasks of life. I become more and more sidelined, and struggle to find a way to be useful or relevant.

I do get better at 'using my words' to describe physical activities to other people. Tying knots and describing how to cast a line are interesting exercises in language use but there are limits, and the frustration is overwhelming when trying to describe things that used to take me seconds to demonstrate. Having led a physical existence, I'm left with few practical ways of passing on a lifetime of physical knowledge. I discover that the fundamental skill of living a life of disability is frustration management.

❖

My friend Berwyn and I go for a drive to stave off the ever-present cabin fever. We end up in the carpark of a country pub which is otherwise empty – there aren't many people around out here. We decide on pies, so she leaves me in the car to go and buy them. Soon afterwards I find I'm getting hot so I open the car door, one of the minor actions of independence I can manage. A cushion I use to prop me up falls out onto the ground.

I look at it. It seems like a long way down. I spend some time eyeing up the cushion and imagining the manoeuvres I'll need to perform in order to pick it up. I consider waiting for assistance, but it seems an obvious challenge. It's only a dropped cushion, for God's sake.

The first thing to do is release the seatbelt, something I always have trouble with. With my left hand I pull some slack into the belt, hold it in my teeth to ease the tension on the buckle and with the tip of the longest finger of my right hand, I stab away at the release button, trying to hit it with enough force to open it. This doesn't work because my fingers just fold up under the effort. I have to regroup, twisting around so I can try pushing it with my better, left hand. My fingernail is a bit long and it's slightly unpleasant, but after a few goes the buckle releases. The belt retracts but, in doing so, catches and pins my arm, so I then have to spend some time extracting it. So far, so good.

I bend forward and reach down towards the cushion and, as I knew it would, my body stiffens in spasm. I wait for it to pass before trying again. I can't reach, nowhere near, and I see I need to reposition. I spend some time wriggling around on my seat, a kind of jerky shuffle that eventually gets my arse closer to the edge, which should make it easier for me to reach down.

My altered position is, however, closer to my point of balance. I come to a point where I need to make a decision. Continuing means risking going further than I'll be able to return from; that I won't possess sufficient core strength to sit back up. Should I fail, I'll be at the start of

a slow-motion collapse out of the car and onto the asphalt. I hesitate.
I look down at the cushion. It looks back at me, egging me on.

I reach slowly downwards, trying to hold enough body tension to
avoid flopping out of the car. The closer I get to the cushion, the greater
the effort becomes and I start to shake with the strain of holding myself
up, even as I near the ground.

I get to the point where I can brush the cushion with the tips of
my fingers but can't get any purchase on the smooth fabric. I'll have to
commit: one quick grab, hoping that the weak scissor-grip thing I can
do with my hand will be enough to secure the prize. If I do it quickly, I
might be able to use some natural rebound, some spasm reflex, to get
me back to a point where I can sit up again.

There are only seconds left to decide before I slump out the door
and I see myself in the classic movie situation, clinging to the crumbling
cliff edge, slowly but inexorably losing grip, the river gorge distant
below me, legs swinging in space. I lunge for the pillow and snag it.
My spasm tightens in response and jerks me back up. I gain the few
centimetres I need to return to the point where I can begin the last
battle, to sit upright.

A few moments later and I've done it – exhausted, trembling and
shaky, but successful – cushion in hand. I haven't fallen from the cliff
into the river, or even out the car door onto the carpark. I feel as if I've
earned that pie. Such is the new look of adventure.

It's not all as bad as that though. My friends look after me. They conjure
up some spectacular outings into the outdoors. I'm carried on poles
down to inaccessible beaches and to the tops of bush-covered islands.
There's much humour and novelty in these outings and I begin to see
that there are possibilities for alternative adventures. Trips like these
are easier for my friends to get their teeth into, by involving themselves
in physical activity and lovely places in nature. I'm grateful for the effort

they put into taking me to these places, but in other aspects of my
life it's harder for them to help.

Friendships become different; there's a removal. I find I can still
talk about climbing, canyoning, skiing, to an extent anyway and there's
plenty else to discuss, but gaps open and never get filled. These are
based on an incomprehension of what I'm going through and yet few
people ask, or ask meaningfully. My friends, physical and outdoorsy to
their cores, can only imagine what it's like for me and there seems to
be an unspoken avoidance of some subjects, as if there's a deep horror
that shouldn't be brought to the surface. People are reluctant to bring
thoughts about others' hardship into their lives, and I get it. I was
like that too.

Despite that, people are generally their normal selves with me,
which is something of a relief, since it makes it harder to sink into the
default position of low-grade depression, and I slowly find it easier to
socialise in a fairly normal way. Dinner parties provide an easily handled
happy place, with discussion usually of the light-hearted variety.
My friends are an erudite and intelligent bunch, but their efforts in
life are focused on getting stuff done – building houses, businesses,
their physical and recreational lives – and although they can talk on a
range of subjects – life-saving medical interventions are popular – I feel
myself needing something else. I get on with exploring other avenues.

Reasoning that reactivation of movement pathways in my body may
be possible if I try hard enough, I give it all I've got by deep-ending
myself at a couple of dance music festivals, the domain of happy,
healthy people celebrating their wonderful lives in a flamboyantly
physical manner. Wobbling around on my standing frame at the back
of the dancefloor is a form of deep masochism. With a head full of
psychoactive drugs, in my mind I pull off the most outrageous dance
moves of my life, which feels great in the moment, but quickly feels
hollow. I later joke that I've advanced to a higher plane in which I've
transcended the actual need to dance (much as I make the same
joke about climbing), but the emptiness stays with me. Dance needs

either the feedback of physicality or else a new attitude I haven't yet developed. Much as between the speakers is my spiritual home, where the outfits and characters are more to my taste, at parties I become the guy who sits around the brazier talking shit. But those parties lose their allure without the excitement of dance and I now mostly socialise in smaller groups, and listen more to music that contains meaning other than getting you to shake your hips.

Among the ongoing process of recovery and improvement, some big life decisions have to be made. My accident has bought hardship to others' lives too, and none more so than Ros, my life partner of many years. It started with the midnight call from the rescue coordination centre, then the ensuing traumatic period when survival was questionable, the dramas of ICU and the long months in hospital. She has had to hold our business together, and learn to look after me and manage the constant presence of support workers and others. Our previous lifestyle has almost totally collapsed, as have all our future plans, so it becomes the hardest decision of my life to decide that I need to carry on without her.

I find it hard to articulate my decision and make a hash of it when I try, producing a mishmash of seeming contradictions: I feel I need to deal with this new life on my own. Somehow I need to make a complex situation more simple. I feel I'm a burden she never asked for, even as she stepped up and wore that burden. I need support more than ever, but I can't accept it from the person closest to me. I need to pull myself up by my own bootstraps, to find the real me again (without really knowing what that means). None of those reasons sound that convincing on their own, and I still don't know for sure, but this is what I did: after twenty-seven years together, for better or worse, in the most difficult and least understood decision of my life, I left Ros.

Despite this underlying drive to somehow start again, to build some new life from scratch, I have no real idea of how to go about it. The ways in which my life has been diminished are obvious, how to expand it less so. I remain focused on my physical programme, out of no more than habit, and carry on with my standard routines, because I'm unsure where to go. I come to realise that there's little of use from my past, that I need to look to the future for some kind of relevance. I see that a future free of restrictions lies not with my body, but my mind. I rationalise that my mind can be as my body once was – free from any particular limits and able to range pretty much anywhere. Self-evident though this seems, truly understanding it takes me a while.

Technology helps. It turns out that even a 76 per cent disabled body is able to drive a vehicle, with the appropriate modifications. A remote control system allows me to lower a hydraulic ramp, roll my power wheelchair into the van, click into a docking mechanism on the floor and drive the van away using hand controls– on public roads, no less. More recently, I've taken possession of a gyroscopically controlled wheelchair, if you can call it that. It reaches speeds of over 20 kilometres an hour and has a certain off-road capability, which opens up a lot of terrain that would normally be out of reach, especially beaches. It is, in fact, quite a bit of fun. The trend towards increasing simplicity in my pre-accident life has been replaced by an embracing of technology; there's never been a better time to be a cripple.

The support I receive from the medical system is very much geared towards improving my physical situation, so I feel that I'm branching off on my own when I start to explore a more cerebral life. My vocational adviser tries to remain polite when I suggest ACC provide some support to study writing. 'Perhaps there's something else that might be more, um, useful in a work sense?' I can see her point, but really, I have nothing to guide me through this situation except instinct. It's taken a while, but it finally occurs to me that I need to look somewhere other than the mountains. I decide to write a book, albeit one with mountains in it.

There are occasional visits back to the spinal ward at Burwood for check-ups, and one of the advantages of this is meeting up with some of the old-timers. Among them are a couple of people who have been injured for a long time. They tell me, separately and surprisingly, that their accidents were the best thing that ever happened to them. It's a notion I'm far from accepting. 'Wouldn't have met my husband' and 'Wouldn't have become a successful artist' were sentiments I heard from their mouths but could in no way relate to. Not yet. But the sentiment plants a seed, and although it seems a nebulous concept – a distant kind of dream – it reminds me that I'm not the first to be here. I realise there's a possibility that, once again, life might be worth it, that the twist that turned my world around, is always just another twist from going somewhere else. But how to encourage the right kind of twist to come along? How to create those new realities?

Removal

Of all the things I miss from my previous life – and there are plenty – there is one thing above all others. While in hospital, I don't go near the mountains for many months. When I return home to Wānaka, I see them from everywhere, but keep my distance for a long while, knowing that when I do decide to return it will be difficult. My first foray, after I've been home for several weeks, is an afternoon drive up the Mātukituki; my next is a drive over the Haast Pass road. Both outings cause me to cry, crushed by the combined beauty and inaccessibility of the mountains; by the feeling that looking out a car window will be the closest I'll ever get to them from now on. I remember this feeling from bus trips earlier in my life, nose pressed against the glass and travelling past something that I would like to stop and explore.

I've gone back to being an observer, to that place I never understood, never wanted to be in.

Still, sitting around and looking at the mountains is something I can't tear myself away from. When I do, my mind's-eye picks out the routes I would take, still looking for ridgelines and buttresses as my preferred features. Although I mentally piece together a route over terrain, the imagination of it is no longer a driver for action, a basis for creation, but more a piece of escapism. I don't indulge in it too often, as it doesn't seem like a good habit to get into, an unfulfilled tease. But from time to time I let myself remember how good it was, and it has become okay. Just not too often.

As a way of coping, I've physically moved away from the mountains, and this has worked to an extent. They now seem less – or somehow differently – meaningful. They no longer affect me in any material way and my life is no longer shaped around them. I spend my time more in the human world, surrounded by the things people make, the things they do. Much of it is fabulous and I'll pursue it, but the world people have constructed is only part of a much greater nature and it's the connection to this that I've lost. It seems a much smaller world.

There are other ways to appreciate nature, of course, albeit a much tamed down version of it, through a focus on the smaller things, an appreciation of the humble. I try to observe the details of the natural world. It's something I've always done, from looking for tiny rugosities on a rockface, the slivers of decent ice within a matrix of rime, the exact spot to stand on a slippery rock, but the joy of being in big nature has largely gone, and the joy was the why of it.

It's this absence of the excitements – the take-your-breath-away moments of exultation –that I really miss. I can and do sit by the river, not far from my house, close my eyes and listen to the water moving. I sit in the shade of trees in my garden and watch the branches move in the wind, the play of light through the leaves. I look for nice places, with greenery and water. I follow the antics of birds, watch insects do their thing. I do this all the time and it helps, but it's not the same, not anywhere near. At least, not yet.

My relationship now with the mountains is more notional – one rooted in what's still out there. What would make me emotionally bereft is the idea that places like the Darrans no longer existed. That would diminish my world and I'm sure I wouldn't be the only one. The wilderness has value in itself, outside any values we place on it, but if we knew there was no big wild world out there, we would feel somehow lessened too. I need it to be there, even if I'll never see it again. The knowledge that there's a spectacular obscure out there soothes me now, as it once excited me. Perhaps that's the true meaning of George Mallory's 'Because it is there.' Without there, where would we go?

There is, of course, somewhere else to go. Now that I'm more deeply involved in a world of people and their doings, I've become aware that, by focusing so intently on adventuring, I'd perhaps been distracted from this part of life. Only now am I learning things that most people seem to have learnt long ago, such as the importance of relationships in our lives, and the attractions of a human-centric world, crazy though it may be sometimes.

I'm still adrift between these two worlds, the natural and the human; kicked out of one, yet to land properly in the other. I still need to find the place to which I relate best. I never had to learn to love the mountains; I just did, right from the beginning. There's much else of worth to find out here in the world, but I'll have to look hard to find it, just as I have to try hard to not be trapped in the sense of loss that threatens to paralyse me.

In my new world, it's less obvious what I should focus on. In the years since the accident, there's been no day of reckoning, no flash of inspiration, no particular moment of clarity to point me in a new direction, and nor do I expect there'll be one. The only real concept that can keep me going is that life will be worth it, or might be. Much of what I valued has gone.

I look now for my adventures in the human world, and it seems that a change is beginning. I now notice, as I never used to, how people behave, what they do too. Many things once obscure to me are starting to reveal themselves.

Moving to the city – a city by the sea – has helped. My friends who live here have a different appreciation of nature. They see the beauty in things I have to try harder with: pastoral landscapes, curated gardens. They are also more attuned to the human world, its physical and social constructs, its creativity. I'm learning from them how to interpret my new environment with a fresh eye – one that doesn't need to compare everything to the mountains.

I'm still compelled to keep in touch with the bigger world. Living on the edge of the ocean means there's somewhere I can go to be closer to the rhythms of the natural world, the vagaries of the elements. I can sit in the weather and feel the north-easterly pull on my hair and be in touch with the tides. I can watch storms raise the sea into rough lines of breakers, and afterwards I can weave my way through the debris washed up on the sand and feel a greater world beyond the horizon. And I'm not the only one on the beach, looking out to sea, feeling the same emotions.

Reflections

It's easy to reflect on the irony of my accident. I'd spent the bulk of my youth without much thought to consequences, and my early alpine career was characterised by near misses. But I learnt; I moved away from the higher mountains and their inherent dangers, and found my place in the alpine rock and landscapes of the deeper south, especially among the granite of the Darrans. I climbed with friends I trusted. I was never reckless, but I had been obsessed, or close to it. My obsessions slowly subsided, I gained knowledge and became safer in the hills all the time. And yet, in the end, despite all that, a root breaks...

So yes, there is a sense of irony but I don't think of it too much; experience might not have saved me on the day, but it has given me perspective. Earlier in my life, my friends died in the mountains. Now they die of medical conditions, and a car smash is a possibility for anyone; life has a random element wherever you are. As well as being one of the unlucky few, I'm also one of the lucky ones. A few millimetres of spinal displacement less and I could be perfectly functional. A few millimetres more, dead.

I asked Richard to read over an early draft of this manuscript. His summation of the main theme – that I finally found the place where it all came together for me and then shit happened – seemed as good as any other. The absolute, definitive cut-off from the nature I lived for, often makes me feel helpless about what to do next, but of everything I've learnt from a life of adventuring, some kind of tolerance seems a good one to bring with me. Acceptance seems the only reasonable response to the consequences of your actions, whatever they might be. Acceptance of consequences, but of all the good times too; acceptance is helping me through the now.

It feels as if there should be other qualities I can use that have come from adventuring. Determination, perseverance, enduring discomfort, might all be relevant to *how* I live my life, but less so to what I live my life *for*. It seems worth persevering only if you can see the possibilities. Those possibilities are less obvious right now, but it probably doesn't matter; I just need to suspect it will be worth it. Pressing on and hoping for the best is something I've done plenty of in the hills, and regardless of whether I made it to the top, it all seemed to work out in the end; it seems a worthwhile thought to carry with me.

I have survived my accident, and reasonably well. Whether my time in the mountains can be credited with any of that – some inherent toughness, some great will to live – I can't say. I have memories of the mountains and they are good ones. Having a life of wildness and nature behind me helps with the now, simply because I have lived. It was worth it at the time; it is still worth it now.

I nearly found the solace of death among the mountains the night of my fall, and it would have had a certain rightness to it, to drift off into the baroque theatre of the storm, surrounded by the mountains of what had become my home ground. However, I'm still here, and living. Most physicality is beyond me now, but there's much to look forward to. Although the high drama of the mountains is gone, I have found things to involve the parts of me that still function. In the long and sometimes lost years since the fall there has been plenty of time to reflect. I can feel, reluctantly, the landscapes of the mountain world receding, I will be forever coming to grips with the human landscape to which I'm now restricted, but I have a secret weapon: I know the thing that has saved me.

Simply put, that thing is people; the beauty and power of my relationships are as apparent to me now, as another beauty once was in the hills. Some friendships have faded away, others have grown stronger and some have transformed into something else. Without people, though, I would be nowhere.

Complete strangers have offered support for the simple reason that they see I need it, and that support has taken many forms: handwritten cards of love, links to the latest scientific advances, the wackiest alternative remedies. Other people in my situation have made contact, offering their stories and experience. It has all helped.

My friends and family have stopped me from withdrawing into myself. My friends – and my support workers number firmly among them – have become expert in getting me up steps, into inaccessible locations, into trouble. I love them for it. They suggest outings and events that have nothing to do with the mountains and they're good. I've become better at going out to music gigs, performance, and entertainment events. I've started to dress more smartly again when I go out, and feel better for doing so. I'm finding life becoming interesting once again. I laugh a lot more.

The mountains affect all our lives to some degree and they've shaped my life. They've given me much, but I've realised something:

the mountains, unlike people, never cared for me. They were glorious companions, and it was an ardent relationship, but ultimately, it was a one-sided affair. My relationship with the mountains was all about me, simply a reflection, no more, no less, of what I allowed myself to give to them. For a while it was everything, and I'm lucky to be here with the memories I have.

From early on – from that first time on Aoraki – it seemed obvious, even wearing the blinkers of obsession, that climbing wasn't about the summit. The mountain journey was worth it in itself, and this journey I'm on now will be worth it too. I've finished with the mountains now, and that's not a bad thing. It's time to move on, and I'm beginning to see how.

The mountains hold one more surprise for me, one I had, in truth, been waiting for. During the Covid-related downturn in tourism numbers, my friend Suz says she wants to see Milford Sound. She'd never been there, it sounds like a good time to go and I would be the perfect guide. Having recently developed the notion that I should say yes to more things, it happens that, five and a half long years since I've felt emotionally able to make the drive to the Darrans, I say yes.

It's much easier than I thought it might be. We travel the Milford road on a beautiful day and the lack of tourist traffic makes the drive more pleasant than ever. The mountains stand clear against the sky, as spectacular as always. We stop at all the roadside viewing bays. I scan the walls and ridges, ascertain some small changes in the snowfields, the odd new rockfall here and there, some flood damage from a recent heavy rain, and feel as though I've never left. I'd expected to at least get a little misty eyed, but am surprised by a feeling of contentment, a feeling of coming home.

It comes to me as something of an epiphany that I don't feel the sadness I'd expected to, and it takes me a while to put my finger on it.

Māori have a concept of tūrangawaewae – a place to stand – more generally taken to mean a place where your roots run deep, to which you feel an essential connection. It occurs to me as we drive through the forest on the way home that this is the source of my contentment: the realisation that I'm part of this place, even as it's part of me. That the Darrans still stand here means that I still stand here too. I drive home, not full of sadness and frustration, but instead feeling as if I've passed in some way, from one life to another. At last.

I close my eyes. I'm sitting within the branches of an old tree. From here I can see further up a valley I know well, to where the bush gives way to more open country. Beyond that, tussock slopes angle up to great walls of rock, some of which rise to snowy heights, some so cold they are streaked with ice, some so high they disappear into cloud. A breeze stirs the tree, moves the branches I stand on, pushes the clouds across the sky. Perhaps, just perhaps, this is how something comes, finally, to an end.

Acknowledgements

As with everything we do, this book would not have been written without the efforts of others, and there's a lot of you. The acknowledgements on this page can only be a small measure of the help I've received and I've separated it out into two specific areas – life since my accident, and help with this book.

In rough chronological order starting from the moment I broke my neck until now:

To Rich, Richard and Tom, my stoic companions through the storm – you saved my life. Just now, words fail me. Then, the Te Anau SAR team got me out of there (also saving my life) before the medical teams at Dunedin Hospital and the ICU at Christchurch Hospital carried on saving my life for a few weeks after my accident. Good job sounds inadequate but I'll say it anyway, along with an exclamation mark and my hearfelt thanks. After that, the entire team at the Burwood Spinal Unit – doctors, nurses, physiotherapists, psychologists, ward staff – almost made it a hard place to leave, even after seven months.

Since then, my support workers have so obviously cared for me that it has made all the difference. You have lifted my spirits (not to mention my wobbly body) and I love you all for it.

To those of you who have bent, strained, massaged and worked my body into it's new form, thank you. Without that body, I would no longer have my mind.

I also feel compelled to give some big ups to the publicly funded ACC system. For all its faults, it has supported me well and continues to do so.

Apart from some early doodlings, I started writing in the first Covid-inspired lockdown of 2020. Not knowing what to do with it, I sent what I'd done to the fabulous Caroline Barron, who put me on track with her very considered manuscript assessment. She can be found at: caroline@carolinebarronauthor.com

Richard Thomson did some early reading and offered several handy suggestions.

Since then Robbie Burton has had the grace to take on publishing it in a particularly positive and constructive manner. My thanks to Robbie and the entire team at Potton and Burton for coming up with such a handsome looking book.

I really enjoyed the editing process and that is due to the efforts of Anna Rogers who has made that journey a pleasure.

Inside you will see the nifty little hand drawn maps from the nimble fingers and mind of Bruce Dowrick.

On the cover you will see the spectacular and evocative art of Diana Adams, who has been gracious enough to provide it. Visit: dianaadamsart@gmail.com.

The back cover endorsement comes from Allan Uren, which just goes to show it's all about who you know...

A VERY BIG thanks to all of you.

Within this book I have included some of the origin stories of Ngai Tahu. This information has mostly been gleaned from the Ngai Tahu website and online videos of Tā Tipene O'Reagan recounting them. I would like to acknowledge their generosity in making them so available.

Several dead people have featured in this book. In order of appearance they are:

Carol Nash
Jeremy Strang
Danny Grziwotz
Gordon Legge
Dave Hiddleston
Russell Braddock

Just because you're dead, doesn't mean you're not still part of my life. There are others of you that died in the mountains as well but you haven't made it into my book. It doesn't mean you are not in my heart though, it's just how it is. Please excuse me.

And of course my greatest debt is to those still living. To all those that wiped my brow, stayed with me at night, made me all that wonderful food and lifted my spirits day after day after day with your help and encouragement – much love.

About the author

For over 30 years Dave Vass was one of New Zealand's leading
mountaineers. During this period he also established and ran
New Zealand's first canyoning business in the foothills of the
Southern Alps near Wānaka.

In 2015 he broke his neck while on a climbing trip in Fiordland,
and has been exploring the potential of a life-form that uses wheels
instead of legs ever since. Dave has written previously for the
New Zealand Alpine Journal and *Climber* magazine. This is his first
book, and since finishing it he has completed an MA in Creative
Writing at the International Institute of Modern Letters in Wellington.
He currently lives in Otautahi/Christchurch, New Zealand.